W9-BVL-249

The Seasonal Kitchen

This edition published in 2012.

Parragon
Queen Street House
4 Queen Street
Bath
BA1 1HE, UK

ISBN: 978-1-4454-4982-1

Printed in China

Notes for the reader:

All spoon measurements are level.

Unless otherwise stated milk is assumed to be whole and eggs are medium-size.

Times given are an approximate guide only. Preparation times differ according to different techniques used by different people and the cooking times may also vary from those given as a result of the type of oven used.

Sufferers from nut allergies should be aware that some of the ready-prepared ingredients used in the recipes in this book may contain nuts. Always check the packaging before use.

Recipes using raw or very lightly cooked eggs should be avoided by infants, the elderly, pregnant women, convalescents, and anyone with a chronic condition.

Contents

Welcome to

The Seasonal Kitchen is a celebration of the fantastic range of fresh produce available to all of us throughout the year. Who doesn't love the taste of locally grown strawberries or the smell of a freshly baked Apple Pie made with apples just picked from the tree? This book contains over 100 of our favorite simple and delicious recipes. From a simple *Penne Pasta* with *Fresh Pesto Sauce*, to *Pumpkin Loaf* and *Poached Salmon*, there's a dish for every occasion.

Here at *Blueberry Hill* we understand that busy families need easy and simple solutions. With our recipes you can still feed your family good, honest, wholesome and nutritious meals but you won't feel like you're tied to your kitchen!

Happy cooking and warmest wishes from all of us at

Blueberry Hill

Pantry Essentials

A well-stocked pantry helps to make life a little easier when trying to plan out what to cook. The ingredients listed below are the things you'll regularly find on our shopping list.

Dry Ingredients

Pasta Spaghetti and macaroni are good basic pastas but for a broader choice add lasagna (sheets), Cannelloni (tubes), fusilli (spirals), farfalle (bows), tagliatelle (ribbons) and conchiglie (shells).

Rice Every pantry should have a good long-grain rice supplemented with basmati rice, risotto rice and brown rice.

Noodles Most noodles are associated with Asian cooking. Make sure you have a selection of both Egg noodles and rice noodles for use in soups and stir-fries.

Flour All-purpose flour is great for thickening casseroles, making sauces and coating food before cooking. Self-rising flour is used for baking whilst bread making generally requires specific bread flour due to higher gluten levels.

Sugar White and brown sugar cover off the basic needs, but some recipes will call for confectioner's sugar for making frostings and for decoration.

Nuts and Seeds Walnuts, almonds, pine nuts and cashews can be used to add extra crunch and texture to savory dishes and baked goods. Make sure to store them in airtight containers. Sesame seeds are useful for many Asian inspired dishes.

Oils & Vinegars

Extra Virgin Olive Oil Ideal for drizzling over salads Extra Virgin Olive Oil is produced from the first cold-pressing of the olives and is a premium olive oil with a peppery, fruity flavor.

Vegetable Oil Made of a blend of various oils this is best used for frying, as it is very greasy.

Peanut Oil Suitable for drizzling, dressings and mayonnaise as well as forms of cooking this is a very versatile oil.

Wine Vinegars Available in many different varieties, mainly red, white and sherry. They can be used for dressings, marinades, and sauces or sprinkled over foods.

Balsamic Vinegar This delicious vinegar is thick, dark and slightly sweet. It is made from grape juice that is aged in barrels over a number of years.

Herbs & Spices

Nothing beats fresh herbs or spices but it's always good to have the following dried herbs and spices to hand.

Chili Powder This powdered mixture of spices includes dried chiles, cumin, coriander and cloves. Use it to flavor soups and stews.

Paprika This spice is made from ground sweet red pepper pods and its flavor can vary from mild, sweet and pungent to fiery hot. It is excellent in salad and as a garnish.

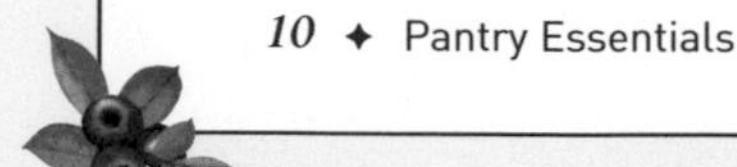

Bay Leaves Originally from the Mediterranean dried bay leaves add a good pungent flavor to soups, sauces and casseroles. They are usually discarded once the food has absorbed their flavor.

Chives Relatives of the onion family these herbs can be added to salads, soups, cream cheese and egg dishes.

Garlic A must for any kitchen fresh cloves of garlic store well or you can buy jars of garlic cloves or dried garlic for your dishes.

Thyme A very versatile herb that can be used with meat, poultry, egg and potato dishes and is also good in soups, sauces, roasts, casseroles and stews.

Five Spice Chinese five spice seasoning is a blend of cloves, cinnamon, fennel seeds, Sichuan peppercorns and Star Anise. It is very popular in stir-fries.

Ginger Dried ginger is particularly good with fruit, cookies and condiments.

Apple Pie Spice This blend of spices usually consists of cinnamon, nutmeg and cardamom. It has a warm, sweet flavor and is delicious in fruit desserts, bread, cakes cookies, pies and drinks.

Other Items

Bouillon Cubes Great for use in casseroles and soups if you do not have time to make or buy fresh stock.

Tomato Paste This is a condensed puree, which adds a more intense flavor in sauces and soups.

Canned Tomatoes Always useful for a variety of dishes, from sauces and soups to stews and casseroles.

Canned Beans Always have a few cans of beans to hand from Red kidney beans, to lentils and chickpeas. They don't require soaking and can be very useful to have in any pantry.

Canned Fish Many dishes can use canned or fresh fish. Tuna, crab and anchovies are all useful for salads or pasta dishes.

Pickled Foods Pickles, pickled onions and capers make perfect accompaniments and garnishes for meat and vegetable dishes.

Olives It's always useful to have a can or a bottle of olives. They are delicious in salads, pastas and on pizzas or to blend and make dips from.

Soy Sauce A popular Chinese sauce it is used within all Asian foods and adds a salty flavor. Soy comes in light and dark varieties use the light one with shellfish and the dark one with duck and meat.

Worcestershire Sauce This spicy sauce adds a fantastic fiery flavor to casseroles and soups.

Spring

Chicken and Mushroom Tagliatelle

serves 4

8 ounces dried shiitake mushrooms

1½ cups hot water

1 tablespoon olive oil

6 bacon strips, chopped

3 skinless, boneless chicken breasts, cut into strips

8 ounces fresh shiitake mushrooms, sliced

1 small onion, finely chopped

1 teaspoon finely chopped fresh oregano or marjoram

1 cup chicken stock

1¼ cups cream

1 pound dried tagliatelle

½ cup freshly grated Parmesan cheese

Salt and pepper

Chopped fresh flat-leaf parsley, to garnish

Put the dried mushrooms in a bowl with the hot water. Let soak for 30 minutes, or until softened. Remove, squeezing excess water back into the bowl. Strain the liquid in a fine-mesh strainer and reserve. Slice the soaked mushrooms, discarding the stems.

Heat the oil in a large skillet over medium heat. Add the bacon and chicken, then cook for about 3 minutes. Add the dried and fresh mushrooms, the onion, and oregano. Cook for 5–7 minutes, or until soft. Pour in the stock and the mushroom liquid. Bring to a boil, stirring. Simmer for about 10 minutes, continuing to stir, until reduced. Add the cream and simmer for 5 minutes, stirring, until beginning to thicken. Season with salt and pepper. Remove the skillet from the heat and set aside.

Meanwhile, bring a large saucepan of lightly salted water to a boil. Add the pasta, bring back to a boil, and cook for 8–10 minutes, or until tender but still firm to the bite. Drain and transfer to a serving dish. Pour the sauce over the pasta. Add half the Parmesan cheese and mix. Sprinkle with parsley and serve with the remaining Parmesan.

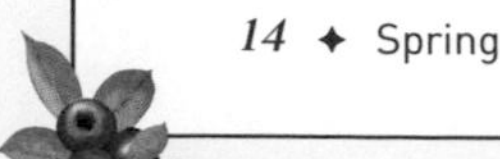

Spring Lamb Stew with Chickpeas

serves 4-6

6 tablespoons olive oil
8 ounces chorizo sausage, cut into ¼-inch thick slices, casings removed
2 large onions, chopped
6 large garlic cloves, crushed
2 pounds boned leg of lamb, cut into 2-inch chunks
1¼ cups lamb stock or water
½ cup red wine
2 tablespoons sherry vinegar
Two 14.5-ounce cans chopped tomatoes
4 sprigs fresh thyme, plus extra to garnish
2 bay leaves
½ teaspoon sweet Spanish paprika
Two 15-ounce cans chickpeas, rinsed and drained
Salt and pepper

Preheat the oven to 325°F.

Heat 4 tablespoons of the oil in a large, heavy-bottom flameproof casserole over medium-high heat. Reduce the heat, add the chorizo, and cook for 1 minute; set aside. Add the onions to the casserole and cook for 2 minutes, then add the garlic and continue cooking for 3 minutes, or until the onions are soft, but not brown. Remove from the casserole and set aside.

Heat the remaining 2 tablespoons of oil in the casserole. Add the lamb chunks in a single layer without overcrowding the casserole, and cook until browned on all sides; work in batches, if necessary.

Return the onion mixture to the casserole with all the lamb. Stir in the stock, wine, vinegar, tomatoes and drained chick peas, and salt and pepper to taste. Bring to a boil, scraping any glazed bits from the bottom of the casserole. Reduce the heat and stir in the thyme, bay leaves, and paprika.

Springtime Spicy Chicken with Vegetables

serves 4

5 tablespoons corn oil
4 chicken pieces
6 tablespoons all-purpose flour
1 onion, chopped
2 celery stalks, sliced
1 green bell pepper, seeded and chopped
2 garlic cloves, finely chopped
2 teaspoons chopped fresh thyme
2 fresh red chiles, seeded and finely chopped
One 14.5-ounce can chopped tomatoes
1¼ cups chicken stock
Salt and pepper
Lamb's lettuce and chopped fresh thyme, to garnish

Heat the oil in a large, heavy-bottom saucepan or flameproof casserole. Add the chicken and cook over medium heat, stirring, for 5–10 minutes or until golden. Transfer the chicken to a plate with a slotted spoon.

Stir the flour into the oil and cook over very low heat, stirring constantly, for 15 minutes, or until light golden. Do not let it burn. Immediately add the onion, celery, and green bell pepper and cook, stirring constantly, for 2 minutes. Add the garlic, thyme, and chiles and cook, stirring, for 1 minute.

Stir in the tomatoes and their juices, then gradually stir in the stock. Return the chicken pieces to the pan, cover, and simmer for 45 minutes, or until the chicken is cooked through and tender. Season to taste with salt and pepper, transfer to warmed serving plates, and serve immediately, garnished with some lamb's lettuce and a sprinkling of chopped thyme.

Pasta with Fresh Pesto

serves 4

1 pound dried tagliatelle

Fresh basil sprigs, to garnish

for the Pesto Sauce

2 garlic cloves

¼ cup pine nuts

2 ½ cups fresh basil leaves

½ cup freshly grated Parmesan cheese

½ cup olive oil

Salt

To make the pesto, put the garlic, pine nuts, a large pinch of salt, and the basil into a mortar, and pound to a paste with a pestle. Transfer to a bowl and gradually work in the cheese with a wooden spoon, followed by the olive oil, to make a thick, creamy sauce. Taste and adjust the seasoning, if necessary.

Alternatively, put the garlic, pine nuts, and a large pinch of salt into a food processor or blender and process briefly. Add the basil leaves and process to a paste. With the motor still running, gradually add the olive oil. Scrape into a bowl and beat in the cheese. Season with salt to taste.

Bring a large saucepan of lightly salted water to a boil. Add the pasta, return to a boil, and cook for 8–10 minutes, or according to the package directions, until tender but still firm to the bite.

Drain the pasta well, return to the pan, and toss with half of the pesto, then divide among warmed serving plates and top with the remaining pesto. Garnish with basil sprigs and serve immediately.

Sunflower Seed Muffins

makes 12 muffins

6 tablespoons canola oil, plus extra for oiling (optional)
1 cup whole-wheat flour
1 tablespoon baking powder
½ cup light brown sugar
2 cups rolled oats
½ cup golden raisins
½ cup sunflower seeds
2 eggs
1 cup skim milk
1 teaspoon vanilla extract

Preheat the oven to 400°F.

Oil a 12-hole muffin pan or line with 12 paper cases. Sift together the flour and baking powder into a large bowl, adding the contents of the strainer back into the bowl. Stir in the sugar, oats, golden raisins, and scant ½ cup of the sunflower seeds.

Lightly beat the eggs in a large pitcher or bowl, then beat in the milk, 6 tablespoons of oil, and vanilla extract. Make a well in the center of the dry ingredients and pour in the beaten liquid ingredients. Stir gently until just combined; do not overmix.

Spoon the batter into the prepared muffin pan. Sprinkle the remaining sunflower seeds over the tops of the muffins. Bake in the preheated oven for about 20 minutes, until well risen, golden brown, and firm to the touch.

Leave the muffins in the pan for 5 minutes to cool slightly, then serve warm or transfer to a wire rack and let cool.

Lemon and Orange Monkfish

serves 8

2 lemons

2 oranges

2 monkfish tails, about 1 pound each, skinned and cut into 4 fillets

8 fresh lemon thyme sprigs

2 tablespoons olive oil

2 tablespoons green peppercorns, lightly crushed

Salt

Cut 8 lemon slices and 8 orange slices, reserving the remaining fruit. Rinse the monkfish fillets under cold running water and pat dry with paper towels. Place the monkfish fillets, cut-side up, on a work surface and divide the citrus slices among them. Top with the lemon thyme.

Tie each fillet at intervals with kitchen string to secure the citrus slices and thyme. Place the monkfish in a large, shallow, nonmetallic dish.

Squeeze the juice from the remaining fruit into a pitcher, add the oil, and mix together. Season to taste with salt, then spoon the mixture over the fish. Cover with plastic wrap and let marinate in the refrigerator for up to 1 hour, spooning the marinade over the fish tails once or twice.

Preheat the broiler. Drain the fish, reserving the marinade. Sprinkle the crushed peppercorns over the fish, pressing them in with your fingers, then cook over medium-high heat, turning and brushing frequently with the marinade, for 20–25 minutes.

Transfer to a cutting board, remove and discard the string, and cut the fish into slices. Serve immediately.

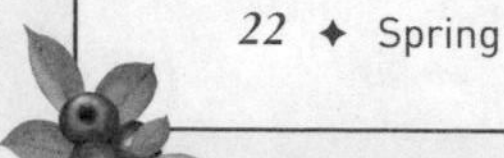

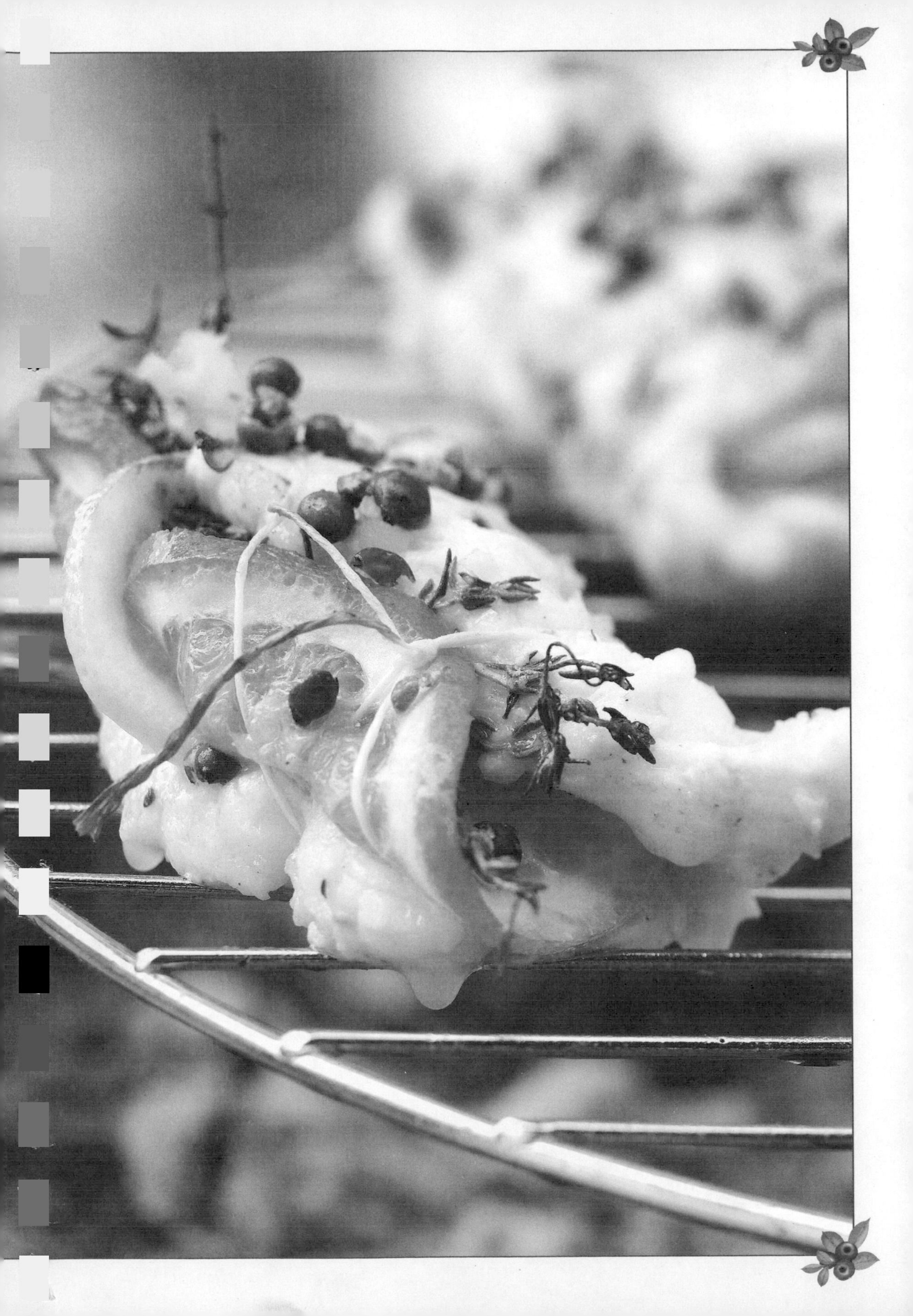

Spring Fresh Salad

serves 4

2 dessert apples
Juice of 1 lemon
Large chunk of watermelon, seeded and cubed
1 head Belgian endive, sliced into rounds
4 sticks celery with leaves, coarsely chopped
1 tablespoon walnut oil

Core and dice the apples. Place in a bowl and pour over the lemon juice. Mix well to prevent discoloration.

Add the rest of the fruit and vegetables to the bowl and mix gently. Pour in the walnut oil, mix again and serve.

Broiled Spring Lamb with Yogurt and Herb Dressing

serves 4

2 tablespoons olive oil, plus extra for broiling
1 tablespoon tomato paste
½ tablespoon ground cumin
1 teaspoon lemon juice
1 garlic clove, crushed
Pinch of cayenne pepper
1 pound 2 ounces lamb shoulder, trimmed, with excess fat removed, and sliced
Salt and pepper
Lightly toasted sesame seeds and fresh parsley sprig, for garnishing

for the dressing

2 tablespoons fresh lemon juice
1 teaspoon good-quality honey
⅓ cup Greek-style yogurt
2 tablespoons finely shredded fresh mint
2 tablespoons chopped fresh parsley
1 tablespoon finely snipped fresh chives
Salt and pepper

Mix the 2 tablespoons oil, tomato paste, cumin, lemon juice, garlic, cayenne, and salt and pepper to taste, together in a nonmetallic bowl. Add the lamb slices and rub all over with the marinade.

Cover the bowl and marinate the lamb in the refrigerator for at least 2 hours, but ideally overnight.

Meanwhile, to make the dressing, whisk the lemon juice and honey together until the honey dissolves. Whisk in the yogurt until well blended. Stir in the herbs and add salt and pepper to taste. Cover and chill until required.

Remove the lamb from the refrigerator 15 minutes before you are ready to cook. Heat the broiler to its highest setting and lightly brush the broil rack with oil. Broil the lamb, turning once, for 10 minutes for medium and 12 minutes for well done. Let the lamb cool completely, then cover and chill until required.

Thinly slice the lamb, then divide among 4 plates. Adjust the seasoning in the dressing, if necessary, then spoon over the lamb slices. To serve, sprinkle with toasted sesame seeds and garnish with the parsley sprig.

Blueberry Crumb Cake

serves 12

2 cups fresh blueberries

3 cups self-rising flour, plus extra for dusting

1¼ teaspoons salt

½ teaspoon apple-pie spice

1¼ cups butter, at room temperature, plus extra for greasing

1¾ cups superfine sugar

½ teaspoon vanilla extract

½ teaspoon almond extract

2 extra-large eggs

1¼– 1½ cups sour cream

for the Almond Streusel Topping

½ cup (1 stick) butter, diced

1 cup all-purpose flour

2 tablespoons firmly packed light brown sugar

1 tablespoon sugar

¼ cup chopped blanched almonds

To make the almond streusel topping, put the butter and flour into a large bowl and rub together until coarse crumbs form. Stir in both types of sugar and the almonds, then let chill in the refrigerator until required.

Preheat the oven to 350°F. Butter a 13 x 9-inch rectangular cake pan and dust with flour. Dust the blueberries with 1 tablespoon of the measured flour and set aside. Sift the remaining flour into a bowl with the salt and apple-pie spice and set aside.

Place the butter in a large bowl and, using an electric mixer, beat until soft and creamy. Add the sugar, vanilla extract, and almond extract and continue beating until the mixture is light and fluffy. Add the eggs, one at a time, beating well after each addition, then beat in 1¼ cups of the sour cream. Beat in the flour until the mixture is soft and falls easily from a spoon. Add the remaining sour cream, 1 tablespoon at a time, if necessary.

Add the blueberries and any loose flour to the batter and quickly fold in. Pour the batter into the prepared pan and smooth the surface. Pinch the streusel topping into large crumbs and scatter evenly over the batter.

Bake the cake in the preheated oven for 45–55 minutes, until it comes away from the side of the pan and a toothpick inserted in the center comes out clean. Transfer the pan to a wire rack and let the cake cool completely. Cut into 12 slices and serve straight from the pan.

Penne with Ham, Tomato and Chili Sauce

serves 4

1 tablespoon olive oil
2 tablespoons butter
1 onion, chopped finely
⅔ cup diced ham
2 garlic cloves, very finely chopped
1 fresh red chile, seeded and finely chopped
Two 14.5-ounce cans canned chopped tomatoes
1 pound dried penne
2 tablespoons chopped fresh flat-leaf parsley
6 tablespoons freshly grated Parmesan cheese
Salt and pepper

Put the olive oil and 1 tablespoon of the butter in a large skillet over medium-low heat. Add the onion and cook for 10 minutes, or until soft and golden.

Add the ham and cook for 5 minutes, or until lightly browned. Stir in the garlic, chile, and tomatoes. Season to taste with salt and pepper. Bring to a boil, then simmer over medium-low heat for 30–40 minutes, or until thickened.

Cook the pasta in plenty of salted boiling water for 8–10 minutes, or until tender but still firm to the bite. Drain and transfer to a warmed serving dish.

Pour the sauce over the pasta. Add the parsley, Parmesan cheese, and the remaining butter. Toss well to mix and serve immediately.

Sourdough Tuna Melts

makes 4 melts

4 slices sourdough bread

Two 5-ounce cans tuna in oil, drained and flaked

4 tablespoons mayonnaise, or to taste

1 tablespoon Dijon mustard or whole-grain mustard, plus extra, to taste

4 scallions, trimmed and chopped

2 tablespoons finely chopped dill pickle or sweet pickle, to taste

1 hard-cooked egg, shelled and finely chopped

1 small carrot, grated

1 tablespoon rinsed and coarsely chopped capers in brine

2 tablespoons chopped parsley or chives

4 large lettuce leaves, such as Romaine

8 thin slices Cheddar cheese

Salt and pepper

Preheat the broiler to high and position the broiler rack about 4 inches from the heat source.

Line a baking sheet with foil and set aside.

Toast the bread under the preheated broiler for 2 minutes on each side, or until crisp and lightly browned.

Meanwhile, put the tuna in a bowl with the mayonnaise and mustard and beat together to break up the tuna. Add the scallions, pickle, egg, carrot, capers, and salt and pepper to taste and beat together, adding extra mayonnaise to taste. Stir in the parsley or chives.

Put the toast on the foil-lined baking sheet and top each slice with a lettuce leaf. Divide the tuna salad among the slices of toast and spread out. Top each sandwich with cheese slices, cut to fit.

Place under the broiler and broil for 2 minutes, or until the cheese is melted and lightly browned.

Cut each tuna melt into four slices, transfer to a plate, and serve.

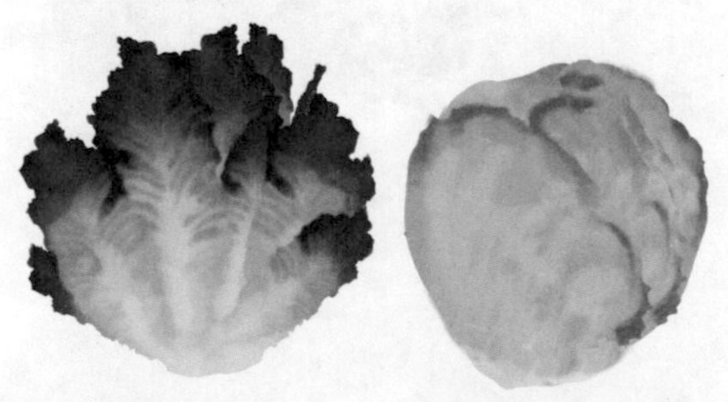

Spaghettini with Chile, Tomatoes and Black Olives

serves 4

1 tablespoon olive oil
1 garlic clove, finely chopped
2 teaspoons bottled capers, drained, rinsed, and chopped
12 black olives, pitted and chopped
½ dried red chile, crushed
Two 14.5-ounce cans chopped tomatoes
1 tablespoon chopped fresh parsley, plus extra to garnish
12 ounces dried spaghettini
2 tablespoons freshly grated Parmesan cheese
Salt and freshly ground black pepper

Heat the olive oil in a large, heavy-bottom skillet. Add the garlic and cook over low heat for 30 seconds, then add the capers, olives, dried chile, and tomatoes, and season to taste with salt. Partially cover the skillet and simmer gently for 20 minutes.

Stir in the parsley, partially cover the skillet again, and simmer for an additional 10 minutes.

Meanwhile, bring a large, heavy-bottom pan of lightly salted water to a boil. Add the pasta, return to a boil, and cook for 8–10 minutes, or until tender but still firm to the bite. Drain and transfer to a warmed serving dish.

Add the tomato and olive sauce and toss well. Sprinkle the Parmesan over the pasta and garnish with extra chopped parsley. Serve immediately.

Spring Onion & Cheese Tartlets

serves 12

for the pie dough

¾ cup all-purpose flour, plus extra for dusting

¼ teaspoon salt

6 tablespoons (¾ stick) butter, cut into small pieces

1–2 tablespoons water

for the filling

1 egg, beaten

⅔ cup light cream

¼ cup grated Cheddar cheese

Scallions, finely chopped

Salt, to taste

Cayenne pepper, to taste

Preheat the oven to 350°F.

To make the dough: Sift the flour and salt into a large bowl. Add the butter and rub in with your fingertips until the mixture resembles breadcrumbs. Stir in the water and mix until a soft dough forms. Shape the dough into a ball, cover with plastic wrap, and chill in the refrigerator for 30 minutes.

Roll out the dough on a lightly floured surface. Using a 3-inch plain biscuit cutter, cut out 12 circles from the dough and use them to line a 12-hole muffin pan.

To make the filling: Beat together the beaten egg, cream, cheese, and scallions in a pitcher. Season to taste with salt and cayenne pepper. Carefully pour the filling mixture into the pastry shells and bake in the preheated oven for 20–25 minutes, or until the filling is just set and the pastry is golden brown. Serve the tartlets warm or cold.

Beef Stir Fry

serves 4

1 teaspoon olive oil

5 ounces grass-fed, free-range beef steak, such as top round (fat removed), cut into thin strips

1 orange bell pepper, seeded and cut into thin strips

4 scallions, trimmed and chopped

1–2 fresh jalapeño chiles, seeded and chopped

2–3 garlic cloves, chopped

1½ cups trimmed and diagonally halved snow peas

4 ounces large portobello mushrooms, sliced

1 teaspoon hoisin sauce, or to taste

1 tablespoon fresh orange juice

Handful arugula or watercress

Heat a wok, then add the oil and heat for 30 seconds. Add the beef and stir-fry for 1 minute, or until browned. Using a slotted spoon, remove and set aside.

Add the bell pepper, scallions, chiles, and garlic and stir-fry for 2 minutes. Add the snow peas and mushrooms and stir-fry for an additional 2 minutes.

Return the beef to the wok and add the hoisin sauce and orange juice. Stir-fry for 2–3 minutes, or until the beef is tender and the vegetables are tender but still firm to the bite. Stir in the arugula or watercress and stir-fry until it starts to wilt. Serve immediately, divided equally among warmed bowls.

Monkfish with Lemon & Parsley Crust

serves 4

4 tablespoons sunflower oil
4 tablespoons fresh breadcrumbs
4 tablespoons chopped fresh parsley, plus extra sprigs to garnish
Zest of 1 large lemon
4 monkfish fillets, about 5–6 ounces each
Salt and pepper

Preheat the oven to 350°F. Mix together the oil, breadcrumbs, parsley, and lemon zest until well combined. Season to taste with salt and pepper.

Place the fish fillets in a large roasting pan.

Divide the breadcrumb mixture among the fish and press it down with your fingers to ensure it covers the fillets.

Bake in the preheated oven for 7–8 minutes, or until the fish is cooked through.

Garnish with parsley sprigs and serve.

Chicken with Pistachios

serves 4

¼ cup chicken stock
2 tablespoons light soy sauce
2 tablespoons dry sherry
3 teaspoons cornstarch
1 egg white, beaten
Pinch of salt
3 tablespoons peanut oil, plus extra if necessary
1 pound skinless chicken breast, cut into strips
1 pound mushrooms, thinly sliced
1 head broccoli, cut into florets
5 ounces bean sprouts
4 ounces canned water chestnuts, drained and thinly sliced
1 cup pistachios, plus extra to garnish
Boiled rice, to serve

Mix the chicken stock, soy sauce, sherry, and 1 teaspoon of the cornstarch together in a bowl. Set aside.

Mix the egg white, salt, 2 tablespoons of the oil, and 2 teaspoons of the cornstarch together in a large bowl. Add the chicken and toss to coat.

Heat a large wok over high heat for 30 seconds. Add the remaining oil, swirl it around to coat the bottom, and heat for 30 seconds. Add the chicken in batches and stir-fry until golden. Remove the chicken from the wok, drain on paper towels, and keep warm.

Add more oil to the wok if needed and stir-fry the mushrooms, then add the broccoli and stir-fry for an additional 2–3 minutes.

Return the chicken to the wok and add the bean sprouts, water chestnuts, and pistachios. Stir-fry until all the ingredients are thoroughly warm. Add the chicken stock mixture and cook, stirring, until thickened. Serve over a bed of rice, garnished with the reserved pistachios.

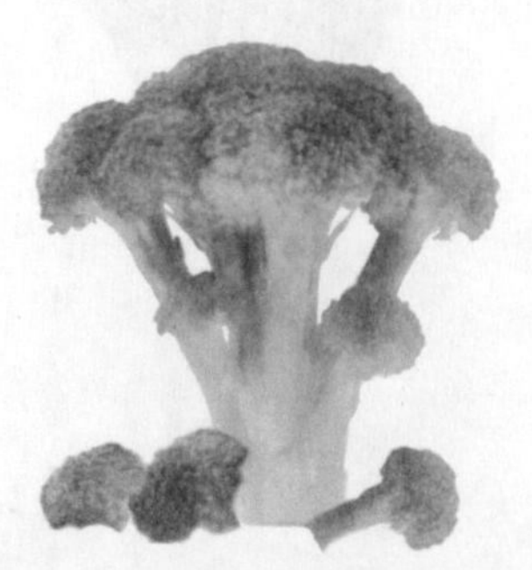

Asparagus & Tomato Salad

serves 4

8 ounces asparagus spears

1 lamb's lettuce, washed and torn

1 handful arugula or mizuna leaves

1 pound ripe tomatoes, sliced

12 black olives, pitted and chopped

1 tablespoon toasted pine nuts

for the dressing

1 teaspoon lemon oil

1 tablespoon olive oil

1 teaspoon whole-grain mustard

2 tablespoons balsamic vinegar

Sea salt and pepper

Steam the asparagus spears for 8 minutes, or until tender. Rinse under cold running water to prevent them cooking any further, then cut into 2-inch pieces.

Arrange the greens around a salad platter to form the base of the salad. Place the sliced tomatoes in a circle on top and the asparagus in the center.

Sprinkle the black olives and pine nuts over the top. Put the lemon oil, olive oil, mustard, and vinegar in a screw-top jar and season to taste with sea salt and black pepper. Shake vigorously and drizzle over the salad.

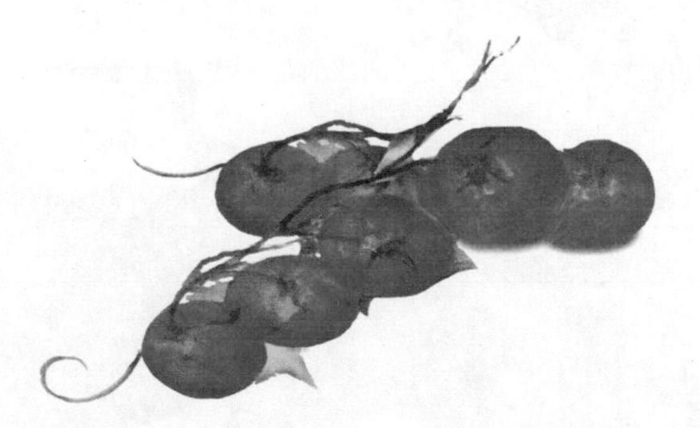

Homemade Granola

serves 6–8

3 cups rolled oats
2 Granny Smith or similar tart apples, peeled and diced
½ cup chopped dried figs
½ cup slivered almonds
2 tablespoons good-quality honey
¼ cup cold water
1 teaspoon ground cinnamon
1 teaspoon vanilla extract
1 teaspoon butter, melted, for greasing
Greek-style yogurt, for serving

Preheat the oven to 325°F.

Mix the oats, apples, figs, and almonds together in a large bowl. Bring the honey, water, cinnamon, and vanilla extract to a boil in a saucepan, then pour over the oat mixture, stirring well to make sure that all the ingredients are coated.

Lightly grease a large baking sheet with the butter and spread the oat mixture out evenly on the sheet. Bake for 40–45 minutes, or until the granola is golden brown, stirring with a fork from time to time to break up any lumps.

Pour onto a clean baking sheet and let cool before storing in an airtight container.

Serve sprinkled over bowls of fresh Greek-style yogurt.

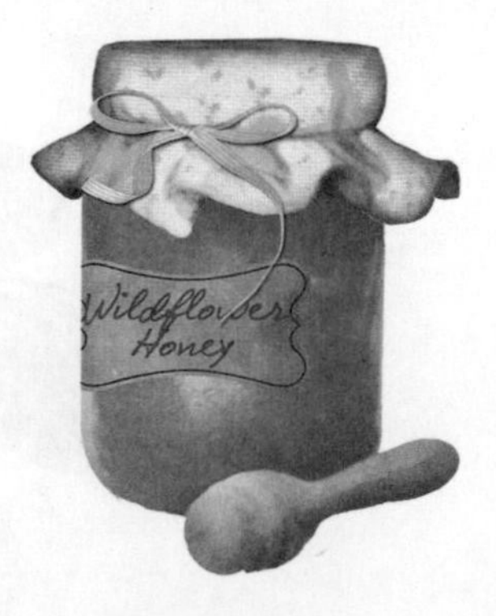

Salmon-Stuffed Potatoes

serves 4

4 large baking potatoes, scrubbed
9 ounces skinless salmon fillet
7 ounces low-fat soft cheese
2–3 tablespoons skimmed milk
2 tablespoons chopped/snipped fresh herbs, such as dill or chives
½ cup grated sharp Cheddar cheese
Salt and pepper

Preheat the oven to 400°F.

Prick the skins of the potatoes and put on the top shelf of the preheated oven. Bake for 50–60 minutes, or until the skins are crisp and the centers are soft when pierced with a sharp knife or skewer.

Meanwhile, lightly poach the salmon fillet in a saucepan of gently simmering water for 4–5 minutes (if in one piece), or until just cooked but still moist. Alternatively, cut into 2–3 equal pieces and cook in a microwave oven on medium heat for 2 minutes, then turn the pieces around so that the cooked parts are in the center and cook for an additional 1 minute, or until just cooked but still moist. Using a fork, flake the flesh into a bowl.

In a separate bowl, blend the soft cheese with just enough of the milk to loosen, then stir in the herbs and a little salt and pepper.

When the potatoes are cooked, preheat the broiler to high. Cut the potatoes in half lengthwise. Carefully scoop the potato flesh out of the skins, reserving the skins, then add to the soft cheese mixture and mash together. Lightly stir in the salmon flakes.

Spoon the filling into the potato skins and top with the cheddar cheese. Cook under the preheated broiler for 1–2 minutes, or until the cheese is bubbling and turning golden. Serve immediately.

Asparagus & Tomato Quiche

serves 4

Butter, for greasing
1 pack frozen prepared pastry
1 bunch thin asparagus spears
9 ounces fresh spinach leaves
3 extra-large eggs, beaten
⅔ cup heavy cream
1 garlic clove, crushed
10 small cherry tomatoes, halved
Handful of fresh basil, chopped
¼ cup grated Parmesan cheese
Salt and pepper

Preheat the oven to 375°F.

Grease a 10 x 12-inch tart pan with butter, then roll out the pastry and line the pan with it.

Cut off any excess dough, prick the bottom with a fork, cover with a piece of wax paper, and fill with dried beans, then bake it in the preheated oven for 20–30 minutes, until lightly browned. Remove from the oven and let cool slightly.

Reduce the oven temperature to 350°F.

Meanwhile, bend the asparagus spears until they snap, and discard the woody ends. Bring a large saucepan of water to a boil, add the asparagus, and blanch for 1 minute, then remove and drain. Add the spinach to the boiling water, cook for 5 minutes then remove and drain very well.

Mix the eggs, cream, and garlic together and season with salt and pepper to taste. Lay the blanched spinach at the bottom of the pastry shell, add the asparagus and tomatoes, cut-side up, in any arrangement you like, scatter over the basil, then pour the egg mixture on top.

Transfer to the oven and bake for about 35 minutes, or until the filling has set. Sprinkle over the Parmesan cheese and let cool to room temperature before serving.

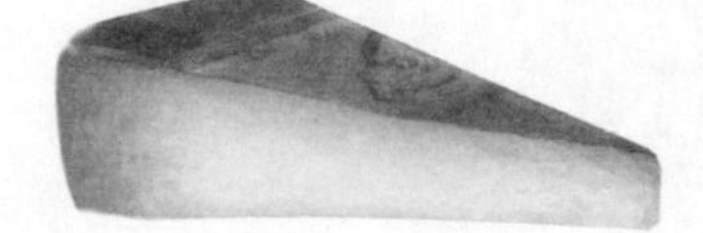

Poached Salmon

serves 6

6–8 pounds salmon (head on)
3 tablespoons salt
3 bay leaves
10 peppercorns
1 onion, peeled and sliced
1 lemon, sliced
Lemon wedges, to serve

Wipe the salmon thoroughly inside and out with paper towels, then use the back of a cook's knife to remove any scales that might still be on the skin. Remove the fins with a pair of scissors and trim the tail. Some people prefer to remove the head, but it is traditionally served with it on.

Place the salmon on a two-handled rack and place in a fish poacher. Fill the poacher with enough cold water to cover the salmon adequately. Sprinkle in the salt, bay leaves, and peppercorns and add the onion and lemon slices.

Place over two low burners and very slowly bring just to a boil.

Cover and simmer very gently. To serve cold, simmer for only 2 minutes, remove from the heat, and cool in the cooking liquid for about 2 hours with the lid on. To serve hot, simmer for 6–8 minutes and let the fish stand in the hot water for 15 minutes before removing. Serve with lemon wedges for squeezing over.

Mixed Herb Omelet

serves 1

3 eggs
2 tablespoons milk
2 tablespoons butter
1 tablespoon chopped herbs
Salt and pepper

Break the eggs into a bowl. Add the milk and salt and pepper to taste, and quickly beat until just blended.

Heat an 8-inch omelet pan or skillet over medium–high heat until very hot and you can feel the heat rising from the surface. Add 2 tablespoons of butter and use a spatula to rub it over the bottom and around the side of the pan as it melts.

As soon as the butter stops sizzling, pour in the eggs. Shake the pan forward and backward over the heat and use the spatula to stir the eggs around the pan in a circular motion. Do not scrape the bottom of the pan.

As the omelet begins to set, use the spatula to push the cooked egg from the edge toward the center, so that the remaining uncooked egg comes in contact with the hot bottom of the pan. Continue doing this for 3 minutes, or until the omelet looks set on the bottom but is still slightly runny on top.

Put the chopped herbs in the center of the omelet. Tilt the pan away from the handle, so that the omelet slides toward the edge of the pan. Use the spatula to fold the top half of the omelet over the herbs. Slide the omelet onto a plate, then rub the remaining butter over the top.

Garnish with the sprig of chervil and serve immediately, accompanied by fresh salad greens.

Tuna & Two-Bean Salad

serves 4

7 ounces green beans

One 14 ounce can small white beans, such as cannellini, rinsed and drained

4 scallions, finely chopped

2 fresh tuna steaks, about 8 ounces, each and ¾ inch thick

Olive oil, for brushing

9 ounces cherry tomatoes, halved

Lettuce leaves

Fresh mint and parsley sprigs, to garnish

Salt and pepper

for the dressing

Handful of fresh mint leaves, shredded

Handful of fresh parsley leaves, chopped

1 garlic clove, crushed

4 tablespoons extra-virgin olive oil

1 tablespoon red-wine vinegar

Salt and pepper

First, make the dressing. Put the mint leaves, parsley leaves, garlic, olive oil, and vinegar into a screw-top jar, add salt and pepper to taste, and shake until blended. Pour into a large bowl and set aside.

Bring a pan of lightly salted water to a boil. Add the green beans and cook for 3 minutes. Add the white beans and cook for another 4 minutes until the green beans are tender-crisp and the white beans are heated through. Drain well and add to the bowl with the dressing and scallions. Toss together.

To cook the tuna, heat a stovetop ridged grill pan over high heat. Lightly brush the tuna steaks with oil, then season to taste with salt and pepper. Cook the steaks for 2 minutes, then turn over and cook on the other side for an additional 2 minutes for rare or up to 4 minutes for well done.

Remove the tuna from the grill pan and leave to rest for 2 minutes, or alternatively leave until completely cool. When ready to serve, add the tomatoes to the bean mixture and toss lightly. Line a serving platter with lettuce leaves and pile on the bean salad. Place the tuna over the top. Serve warm or at room temperature, garnished with the herbs.

Black Pepper Monkfish

serves 4

3 tablespoons cracked black peppercorns

Sea salt

1 pound 5 ounces monkfish fillet, cubed

1 tablespoon light olive oil

for the sauce

1 tablespoon light olive oil

1 shallot, finely chopped

1 garlic clove, finely chopped

3 tablespoons white wine

⅓ cup plain Greek-style yogurt

1 level teaspoon cornstarch

2 tablespoons coarse-grain mustard

2 tablespoons chopped fresh dill

Combine the cracked peppercorns with a little flaked sea salt and press the mixture into the monkfish pieces to coat.

To make the sauce, heat the oil in a small skillet. Add the shallot and stir-fry over medium heat for 3 minutes, until softened. Add the garlic and stir-fry for another 1 minute. Add the wine and cook until evaporated. Stir in the yogurt and cornstarch and bring to a simmer, then add the mustard, dill, and a little salt.

Heat the oil in a skillet until very hot. Add the monkfish cubes and cook for 3 minutes, turning during cooking so that each side is cooked. The fish is ready when the pieces are just firm when pressed. Remove with a slotted spoon and drain on paper towels. Serve with the sauce.

Lamb with Pears

serves 4

1 tablespoon olive oil
2 pounds best end-of-neck lamb cutlets, trimmed of visible fat
6 pears, peeled, cored, and cut into quarters
1 teaspoon ground ginger
4 potatoes, diced
4 tablespoons hard cider (optional)
1 pound green beans
Salt and pepper
2 tablespoons snipped fresh chives, to garnish

Preheat the oven to 325°F.

Heat the olive oil in a flameproof casserole over medium heat. Add the lamb and cook, turning frequently, for 5–10 minutes, or until browned on all sides.

Arrange the pear pieces on top, then sprinkle over the ginger. Cover with the potatoes. Pour in the cider and season to taste with salt and pepper. Cover and cook in the preheated oven for 1¼ hours.

Trim the stem ends of the green beans. Remove the casserole from the oven and add the beans, then re-cover and return to the oven for an additional 30 minutes. Taste and adjust the seasoning and sprinkle with the chives. Serve immediately.

Fusilli with Zucchini & Lemon

serves 4

6 tablespoons olive oil
1 small onion, very thinly sliced
2 garlic cloves, very finely chopped
2 tablespoons chopped fresh rosemary
1 tablespoon chopped fresh flat-leaf parsley
1 pound small zucchini, cut into 1½-inch lengths
Zest of 1 lemon
1 pound dried fusilli (pasta spirals)
Salt and pepper
Freshly grated Parmesan cheese, to serve

Heat the olive oil in a large skillet over medium-low heat. Add the onion and cook gently, stirring occasionally, for about 10 minutes, or until golden.

Raise the heat to medium-high. Add the garlic, rosemary, and parsley. Cook for a few seconds, stirring.

Add the zucchini and lemon rind. Cook for 5–7 minutes, stirring occasionally, until the zucchini are just tender. Season to taste with salt and pepper. Remove from the heat.

Bring a large saucepan of lightly salted water to a boil. Add the pasta, bring back to a boil, and cook for 8–10 minutes, or until tender but still firm to the bite. Drain and transfer to a warmed serving dish.

Briefly reheat the zucchini sauce. Pour over the pasta and toss well to mix. Sprinkle with the Parmesan and serve immediately.

Penne with Mixed Beans

serves 4

1 tablespoon olive oil
1 onion, chopped
1 garlic clove, finely chopped
1 carrot, finely chopped
1 celery stalk, finely chopped
One 15-ounce can mixed beans, drained and rinsed
1 cup strained tomatoes
1 tablespoon chopped fresh chervil, plus extra leaves to garnish
12 ounces dried penne
Salt and pepper

Heat the olive oil in a large, heavy-bottom skillet. Add the onion, garlic, carrot, and celery, and cook over low heat, stirring occasionally, for 5 minutes, or until the onion has softened.

Add the mixed beans, strained tomatoes, and chopped chervil to the skillet, and season the mixture to taste with salt and pepper. Cover and simmer gently for 15 minutes.

Meanwhile, bring a large, heavy-bottom pan of lightly salted water to a boil. Add the pasta, return to a boil, and cook for 8–10 minutes, or until tender but still firm to the bite. Drain the pasta and transfer to a warmed serving dish.

Add the mixed-bean sauce, toss well, and serve immediately, garnished with extra chervil.

Walnut and Seed Bread

makes 2 large loaves

4 cups whole-wheat flour
4 cups multigrain flour
1 cup white bread flour, plus extra for dusting
2 tablespoons sesame seeds
2 tablespoons sunflower seeds
2 tablespoons poppy seeds
1 cup chopped walnuts
2 teaspoons salt
½ ounce active dry yeast
2 tablespoons olive oil or walnut oil
3 cups lukewarm water
1 tablespoon melted butter or oil, for greasing

In a mixing bowl, combine the flours, seeds, walnuts, salt, and yeast. Add the oil and lukewarm water and stir well to form a soft dough.

Turn the dough out onto a lightly floured board and knead well for 5–7 minutes. The dough should have a smooth appearance and feel elastic.

Return the dough to the bowl, cover with a clean dish towel or plastic wrap, and leave in a warm place for 1–1½ hours to rise.

When the dough has doubled in size, turn it out onto a lightly floured board and knead again for 1 minute.

Grease two 2-pound loaf pans well with melted butter or oil. Divide the dough into two. Shape one piece into a rectangle the length of the pan and three times the width. Fold the dough into three lengthwise. Place in one of the pans with the seam underneath for a well-shaped loaf. Repeat with the other piece of dough.

Cover and leave to rise again in a warm place for about 30 minutes, until the bread is well risen above the pans. Meanwhile, preheat the oven to 450°F.

Bake in the center of the preheated oven, for 25–30 minutes. If the loaves are getting too brown, reduce the temperature to 425°F. To test that the bread is cooked, tap the loaf on the base—it should sound hollow.

Cool on a cooling rack for 30 minutes to 1 hour; this enables the steam to escape and prevents a soggy loaf.

Burritos

serves 6

8 ounces dried black beans
2 tablespoons vegetable oil, plus extra for brushing
1 large onion, chopped
2 garlic cloves, finely chopped
1 red bell pepper, seeded and chopped
1 pound 4 ounces ground beef
1 tablespoon ground cumin
1 teaspoon paprika
¼ teaspoon cayenne pepper
Pinch of dried oregano
2 tablespoons ketchup
½ cup red wine
One 14.5-ounce can chopped tomatoes
1 bay leaf
3 tablespoons chopped pickled jalapeño chiles
1 tablespoon chopped fresh cilantro
12 flour tortillas
⅔ cup grated Cheddar cheese
Salt
Guacamole and salsa, to serve

Soak the beans overnight in a bowl of cold water, then drain. Put the beans into a large pan and pour in water to cover. Bring to a boil and boil vigorously for 15 minutes, then drain, rinse, and return to the pan. Add fresh water to cover and bring to a boil. Reduce the heat, cover, and simmer for 1–1½ hours, until tender, then drain.

Preheat the oven to 350°F.

Heat the oil in a large pan. Add the onion, garlic, and bell pepper and cook over low heat, stirring occasionally, for 5 minutes, until softened. Add the ground beef, increase the heat to medium, and cook, stirring frequently and breaking it up with a wooden spoon, for 8–10 minutes, until evenly browned. Reduce the heat, stir in the spices, oregano, and ketchup, and season to taste with salt. Add the wine, tomatoes, bay leaf, and beans and mix well. Cover and simmer, stirring occasionally, for 25 minutes. Stir in the jalapeño chiles and cilantro, and remove from the heat. Remove and discard the bay leaf.

Brush a large ovenproof dish with oil. Using a slotted spoon, divide the ground beef mixture among the tortillas and roll up. Put them in the prepared dish, seam-side down, and sprinkle with the cheese. Bake in the preheated oven for 15 minutes. Serve immediately with guacamole and salsa.

Sweet and Sour Vegetables with Cashews

1 tablespoon peanut oil
1 teaspon chili oil
2 onions, sliced
2 carrots, peeled and thinly sliced
2 zucchini, thinly sliced
4 ounces broccoli, cut into florets
4 ounces button mushrooms, sliced
4 ounces small bok choy, halved
1 tablespoon light brown sugar
2 tablespoons light soy sauce
1 tablespoon rice vinegar
⅓ cup toasted cashews

Heat both oils in a large skillet. Add the onions and stir-fry over medium heat for 1–2 minutes, or until they start to soften.

Add the carrots, zucchini, and broccoli and stir-fry for an additional 2–3 minutes. Add the mushrooms, bok choy, sugar, soy sauce, and vinegar and stir-fry for 1–2 minutes.

Sprinkle the toasted cashews over the stir-fry, and serve immediately.

Sweet & Sour Red Cabbage

serves 6-8

1 head red cabbage
2 tablespoons olive oil
2 onions, finely sliced
1 garlic clove, chopped
2 small baking apples, peeled, cored, and sliced
2 tablespoons light brown sugar
½ teaspoon ground cinnamon
1 teaspoon crushed juniper berries
whole nutmeg, for grating
2 tablespoons red-wine vinegar
Juice of 1 orange
Zest of 1 orange
2 tablespoons cranberry jelly
Salt and pepper

Cut the cabbage into quarters, remove and discard the central stalk, and finely shred.

Heat the oil in a large saucepan and add the cabbage, onions, garlic, and apples. Sprinkle over the sugar, cinnamon, and juniper berries, and grate one-quarter of the nutmeg into the pan.

Pour over the vinegar and orange juice and add the orange rind. Stir well and season with salt and pepper to taste.

Cook over medium heat, stirring occasionally, until the cabbage is just tender but still has "bite." This will take 10–15 minutes, depending on how finely the cabbage is sliced.

Stir in the cranberry jelly and add more salt and pepper, if necessary. Serve hot.

Summer

Spaghetti with Clams

serves 4

2 pounds live clams, scrubbed
¾ cup water
¾ cup dry white wine
12 ounces dried spaghetti
5 tablespoons olive oil
2 garlic cloves, finely chopped
4 tablespoons chopped fresh flat-leaf parsley
Salt and pepper

Discard any clams with broken shells or any that refuse to close when tapped. Place the clams in a large, heavy-bottom pan. Add the water and wine, then cover and cook over high heat, shaking the pan occasionally, for 5 minutes, or until the shells have opened. Remove the clams with a slotted spoon and strain the liquid through a cheesecloth-lined strainer into a small pan. Bring to a boil and cook until reduced by about half. Discard any clams that remain closed and remove the remainder from their shells.

Bring a large, heavy-bottom pan of lightly salted water to a boil. Add the pasta, return to a boil, and cook for 8–10 minutes, or until tender but still firm to the bite.

Meanwhile, heat the olive oil in a large, heavy-bottom skillet. Add the garlic and cook, stirring frequently, for 2 minutes. Add the parsley and the reduced cooking liquid and simmer gently.

Drain the pasta and add it to the skillet with the clams. Season to taste with salt and pepper and cook, stirring constantly, for 4 minutes, or until the pasta is coated and the clams have heated through. Transfer to a warmed serving dish and serve immediately.

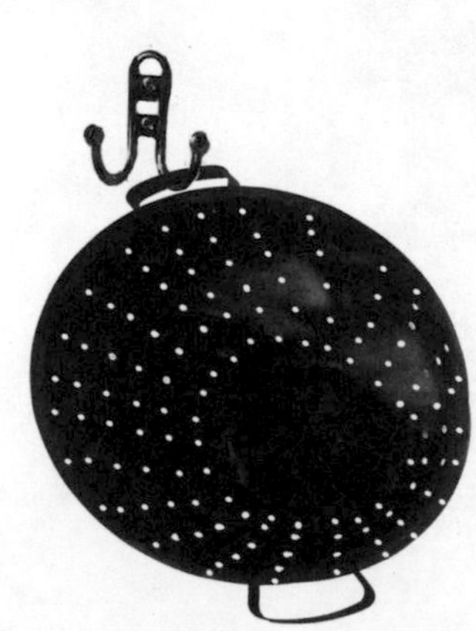

Olive, Bell Pepper & Tomato Pasta

serves 4

8 ounces dried penne
2 tablespoons olive oil
2 tablespoons butter
2 garlic cloves, crushed
1 green bell pepper, seeded and thinly sliced
1 yellow bell pepper, seeded and thinly sliced
16 cherry tomatoes, halved
1 tablespoon chopped fresh oregano, plus extra sprigs to garnish
½ cup dry white wine
2 tablespons quartered, pitted black olives
Two large handfuls arugula
Salt and pepper

Bring a large, heavy-bottom pan of lightly salted water to a boil. Add the pasta, return to a boil, and cook for 8–10 minutes, or until tender but still firm to the bite. Drain the pasta thoroughly.

Heat the oil and butter in a skillet until the butter melts. Cook the garlic for 30 seconds. Add the peppers and cook, stirring constantly, for 3–4 minutes.

Stir in the cherry tomatoes, oregano, wine, and olives, and cook for 3–4 minutes. Season well with salt and pepper and stir in the arugula until just wilted. Transfer the pasta to a serving dish, spoon over the sauce, and garnish with oregano sprigs. Serve.

Mussels with Mustard and Shallots

serves 4

4 pounds live mussels, scrubbed and debearded
3 tablespoons canola oil
½ tablespoon black mustard seeds
8 shallots, chopped
2 garlic cloves, crushed
2 tablespoons distilled vinegar
4 small fresh red chiles
1¾ cups low-fat coconut milk
10 fresh or 1 tablespoon dried curry leaves
½ teaspoon ground turmeric
½ teaspoon chili powder
Salt

Discard any mussels with broken shells or any that refuse to close when tapped with a knife.

Heat the oil in a large skillet or wok with a lid over medium-high heat. Add the mustard seeds and stir them around for about 1 minute, or until they start to pop.

Add the shallots and garlic and cook, stirring frequently, for 3 minutes, or until they start to brown. Stir in the vinegar, whole chiles, coconut milk, curry leaves, turmeric, chili powder, and a pinch of salt and bring to a boil, stirring.

Reduce the heat to very low. Add the mussels, cover the skillet, and leave the mussels to simmer, shaking the pan frequently, for 3–4 minutes, or until they are all open.

Discard any mussels that remain closed. Ladle the mussels into 4 deep serving bowls, spoon over the broth, and serve.

Fried Chicken Wings

serves 4

12 chicken wings
1 egg
½ cup milk
4 tablespoons all-purpose flour
1 teaspoon paprika
2 cups breadcrumbs
4 tablespoons butter
Salt and pepper

Preheat the oven to 425°F.

Separate the chicken wings into 3 pieces each. Discard the bony tip. Beat the egg with the milk in a shallow dish. Combine the flour, paprika, and salt and pepper to taste in a separate shallow dish. Place the breadcrumbs in another shallow dish.

Dip the chicken pieces into the egg to coat well, then drain and roll in the seasoned flour. Remove, shaking off any excess, then roll the chicken in the breadcrumbs, gently pressing them onto the surface and shaking off any excess.

Put the butter in a shallow roasting pan large enough to hold all the chicken pieces in a single layer, then put in the preheated oven to melt. Remove from the oven and arrange the chicken, skin-side down, in the pan and bake in the oven for 10 minutes. Turn and bake for an additional 10 minutes, or until the chicken is tender and the juices run clear when a skewer is inserted into the thickest part of the meat.

Remove the chicken from the pan and arrange on a large warmed platter. Serve hot or at room temperature.

Classic Coleslaw

serves 12

2 pounds thinly sliced green cabbage

2 carrots, peeled, grated or finely julienned on a vegetable slicer

½ cup pineapple juice

1 cup mayonnaise

2 teaspoons sugar

¼ teaspoon cayenne pepper, or to taste

Salt and pepper

Place the cabbage and carrot in a large mixing bowl. In a smaller bowl, whisk together the rest of the ingredients. Taste and adjust the sweetness and spiciness if so desired. Pour over the cabbage mixture and toss until coated.

Dress salad within 30 minutes of serving so it stays crisp and fresh.

Taste for seasoning and toss again right before serving.

Stuffed Red Bell Pepper with Basil

serves 4

¾ cup long-grain brown basmati rice
4 large red bell peppers
2 tablespoons olive oil
1 garlic clove, chopped
4 shallots, chopped
1 celery stalk, chopped
3 tablespoons chopped walnuts
2 tomatoes, peeled and chopped
1 tablespoon lemon juice
⅓ cup raisins
4 tablespoons freshly grated Cheddar cheese (optional)
2 tablespoons chopped fresh basil
Salt and pepper

Preheat the oven to 350°F.

Cook the rice in a saucepan of lightly salted boiling water for 35 minutes. Drain, rinse under cold running water, then drain again.

Meanwhile, using a sharp knife, cut the tops off the bell peppers and set aside. Remove the seeds and white cores, then blanch the bell peppers and reserved tops in boiling water for 2 minutes. Remove from the heat and drain well.

Heat half the oil in a large skillet. Add the garlic and shallots and cook, stirring, for 3 minutes. Add the celery, walnuts, tomatoes, lemon juice, and raisins and cook for an additional 5 minutes. Remove from the heat and stir in the rice, cheese (if using), chopped basil, and seasoning.

Stuff the bell peppers with the rice mixture and arrange them in a baking dish. Place the tops on the bell peppers, drizzle over the remaining oil, loosely cover with foil, and bake in the preheated oven for 45 minutes. Remove from the oven and serve.

Gazpacho

serves 4

9 ounces white bread slices, crusts removed
1 pound 9 ounces tomatoes, peeled and chopped
3 garlic cloves, coarsely chopped
2 red bell peppers, seeded and chopped
1 cucumber, peeled, seeded, and chopped
5 tablespoons extra-virgin olive oil
5 tablespoons red-wine vinegar
1 tablespoon tomato paste
9½ cups water
Salt and pepper
4 ice cubes, to serve

Tear the bread into pieces and place in a blender. Process briefly to make breadcrumbs and transfer to a large bowl. Add the tomatoes, garlic, bell peppers, cucumber, olive oil, vinegar, and tomato paste. Mix well.

Working in batches, place the tomato mixture with about the same amount of the measured water in the food processor or blender and process to a purée. Transfer to another bowl. When all the tomato mixture and water have been blended together, stir well and season to taste with salt and pepper. Cover with plastic wrap and chill in the refrigerator for at least 2 hours, but no longer than 12 hours.

When ready to serve, pour the soup into chilled serving bowls and float an ice cube in each bowl.

Spaghetti with Crab

serves 4

1 dressed crab, about 1 pound including the shell

12 ounces dried spaghetti

6 tablespoons extra-virgin olive oil

1 fresh red chile, seeded and finely chopped

2 garlic cloves, finely chopped

3 tablespoons chopped fresh parsley

2 tablespoons lemon juice

1 teaspoon lemon zest

Salt and pepper

Lemon wedges, to garnish

Using a knife, scoop the meat from the crab shell into a bowl. Mix the white and brown meat lightly together and set aside.

Bring a large pan of lightly salted water to a boil over medium heat. Add the pasta and cook for about 8–10 minutes, or until tender but still firm to the bite. Drain thoroughly and return to the pan.

Meanwhile, heat 2 tablespoons of the oil in a skillet over low heat. Add the chile and garlic and cook for 30 seconds, then add the crabmeat, parsley, lemon juice, and lemon rind. Cook for an additional minute, or until the crabmeat is just heated through.

Add the crab mixture to the pasta with the remaining oil and season to taste with salt and pepper. Toss together thoroughly, then transfer to a large, warmed serving dish. Garnish with a few lemon wedges and serve immediately.

Homemade Hamburgers

serves 6

2 pounds ground beef
1 small onion, grated
1 tablespoon chopped fresh parsley
2 teaspoons Worcestershire sauce
2 tablespoons sunflower oil
Salt and pepper

to serve

6 hamburger buns, split and toasted
Salad greens
Tomato slices
Dill pickles, sliced
Ketchup

Put the ground beef, onion, parsley, and Worcestershire sauce into a bowl, season with salt and pepper to taste, and mix well with your hands until thoroughly combined.

Divide the mixture into 6 equal portions and shape each into a ball, then gently flatten into a hamburger shape. If you have time, chill in the refrigerator for 30 minutes to firm up.

Heat the oil in a large skillet. Add the hamburgers, in batches, and cook over medium heat for 5–8 minutes on each side, turning them carefully with a spatula. Remove from the skillet and keep warm while you cook the remaining hamburgers.

Serve in toasted hamburger buns with salad greens, tomato slices, dill pickles, and ketchup.

Banana and Strawberry Smoothie

serves 2

1 just ripe banana, sliced

¾ cup hulled strawberries

⅔ cup plain yogurt

Put the banana, strawberries, and yogurt into a food processor or blender and process for a few seconds until smooth.

Pour into glasses and serve at once.

Butterfly Cupcakes

makes 12 cupcakes

¾ cup self-rising flour
½ teaspoon baking powder
½ cup (1 stick) butter, softened
½ cup sugar
2 eggs, beaten
Zest of ½ lemon
2–4 tablespoons whole milk
Confectioners' sugar, for dusting

for the filling
4 tablespoons butter
1 cup confectioners' sugar
1 tablespoon lemon juice

Preheat the oven to 375°F.

Place 12 paper liners in a muffin pan. Sift the flour and baking powder into a bowl. Add the butter, sugar, eggs, lemon zest, and enough milk to give a medium-soft consistency.

Beat thoroughly until smooth. Divide the batter among the paper liners and bake in the preheated oven for 15–20 minutes, or until well risen and golden.

To make the filling, place the butter in a bowl, then sift in the sugar and add the lemon juice. Beat well until smooth and creamy. When the cakes are completely cooled, use a sharp-pointed vegetable knife to cut a circle from the top of each cake, then cut each circle in half.

Spoon a little of the buttercream into the center of each cake and press the two semicircular pieces into it to resemble wings. Dust the cakes with confectioners' sugar before serving.

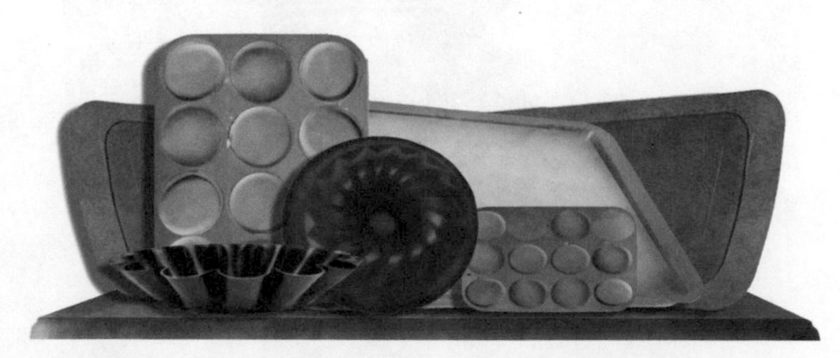

Classic Strawberry Jelly

makes about 1½ cup

3 pounds 5 ounces whole strawberries, hulled and rinsed

2 freshly squeezed lemons, juice strained

7½ cups sugar

1 teaspoon butter

Place the strawberries in a large pan with the lemon juice, then simmer over gentle heat for 15–20 minutes, stirring occasionally, until the fruit has collapsed and is very soft.

Add the sugar and heat, stirring occasionally, until the sugar has completely dissolved. Add the butter, then bring to a boil and boil rapidly for 10–20 minutes, or until the setting point is reached.

Let cool for 8–10 minutes, then skim. Put into warmed sterilized jars and cover the tops with wax disks. When completely cold, cover with cellophane or lids, then label and store in a cool place.

Icebox Cookies

makes about 56 cookies

$2\frac{1}{3}$ cups all-purpose flour

2 tablespoons unsweetened cocoa

½ teaspoon baking soda

1 teaspoon ground ginger

½ teaspoon ground cinnamon

½ cup molasses

4 tablespoons boiling water

½ cup (1 stick) butter, softened

4 tablespoons super fine sugar

Confectioners' sugar, for dusting

Sift the flour, cocoa, baking soda, ginger, and cinnamon together into a bowl, then set aside. Mix the molasses with the water and set aside.

Put the butter into a large bowl and beat with an electric mixer until creamy. Slowly add the superfine sugar and continue beating until light and fluffy. Gradually add the flour mixture, alternating it with the molasses mixture to form a soft dough.

Scrape equal amounts of the dough onto two pieces of plastic wrap and roll into logs, using the plastic wrap as a guide, each about 7 inches long and 2 inches thick. Put the dough logs in the refrigerator for 2 hours, then transfer to the freezer for at least 2 hours and up to 2 months.

When ready to bake, preheat the oven to 350°F and line one or two baking sheets, depending on how many cookies you are baking, with nonstick parchment paper. Unwrap the dough, trim the ends, and cut off ¼ inch slices. Rewrap any unused dough and return to the freezer.

Place the dough slices on the prepared cookie sheet(s) and bake in the preheated oven for 12 minutes. Let cool on the cookie sheet(s) for 3 minutes, then transfer to wire racks, dust with Confectioners' sugar, and let cool completely.

Corn Relish

makes about 2½ cups

5 corn cobs, husked
1 red bell pepper, seeded and finely diced
2 celery stalks, very finely chopped
1 red onion, finely chopped
½ cup plus 2 tablespoons sugar
1 tablespoon salt
2 tablespoons dry mustard
½ teaspoon celery seeds
Small pinch of turmeric (optional)
1 cup apple-cider vinegar
½ cup water

Bring a large saucepan of lightly salted water to a boil, and fill a bowl with iced water. Add the corn to the boiling water, return to a boil, and boil for 2 minutes, or until the kernels are tender-crisp. Using tongs, immediately plunge the cobs into the cold water to halt cooking. Remove the cobs from the water and cut off the kernels, then set aside.

Add the bell pepper, celery, and onion to the corn cooking water, return to a boil, and boil for 2 minutes, or until tender-crisp. Drain well and return to the pan with the corn kernels.

Put the sugar, salt, mustard, celery seeds, and turmeric, if using, into a bowl and mix together, then stir in the vinegar and water. Add to the pan, bring the liquid to a boil, then reduce the heat and simmer for 15 minutes, stirring occasionally.

Ladle the relish into hot, sterilized preserving jars, filling them to within 1½ inch of the top of each jar. Wipe the rims and secure the lids. Let the relish cool completely, then refrigerate for up to 2 months.

Spaghetti with Tuna & Parsley

serves 4

1 pound dried spaghetti
2 tablespoons butter
One 6-ounce can tuna in oil, drained
One 2-ounce can anchovies, drained
1 cup olive oil
1 cup coarsely chopped fresh flat-leaf parsley
⅔ cup sour cream or yogurt
Salt and pepper

Bring a large, heavy-bottom pan of lightly salted water to a boil. Add the spaghetti, return to a boil, and cook for 8–10 minutes, or until tender but still firm to the bite. Drain the spaghetti in a colander and return to the pan. Add the butter, toss thoroughly to coat, and keep warm until needed.

Flake the tuna into smaller pieces using 2 forks. Place the tuna in a food processor or blender with the anchovies, olive oil, and parsley and process until the sauce is smooth. Pour in the sour cream and process for a few seconds to blend. Taste the sauce and season with salt and pepper, if necessary.

Shake the pan of spaghetti over medium heat for a few minutes, or until it is thoroughly warmed through.

Pour the sauce over the spaghetti and toss quickly, using 2 forks. Serve immediately.

Barbecued Chicken

serves 4

2 spring chickens, about 2 pounds each, cut in half

4 tablespoons olive oil

for the barbecue sauce

2 tablespoons butter

2 tablespoons olive oil

1 onion, finely chopped

2 garlic cloves, finely chopped

1 celery stalk, finely chopped

½-inch piece fresh ginger, finely chopped

One 14.5-ounce can chopped tomatoes

2 tablespoons tomato paste

1 tablespoon Worcestershire sauce

2 tablespoons red-wine vinegar

2 tablespoons lemon juice

1 tablespoon brown sugar

1 teaspoon dried oregano

1 bay leaf

Pinch of grated nutmeg

2 tablespoons water

Salt and pepper

First, make the sauce. Melt the butter with the oil in a pan. Add the onion, garlic, celery, and ginger and cook over low heat, stirring occasionally, for 5 minutes, until softened. Stir in the tomatoes, tomato paste, Worcestershire sauce, vinegar, lemon juice, sugar, oregano, bay leaf, nutmeg, and water and season to taste with salt and pepper. Increase the heat to medium and bring to a boil, then reduce the heat and simmer, stirring occasionally, for 30–40 minutes, until thickened.

Meanwhile, preheat the barbecue or broiler. Brush the skin sides of the chicken halves with half the oil and put them skin-side down on the barbecue grill or skin-side uppermost on the broiler rack. Cook on the barbecue or under the preheated broiler for 10 minutes, then brush with the remaining oil, turn them over, and cook for an additional 20 minutes, until golden brown.

Brush the chicken with half the sauce. Continue to cook, turning and brushing frequently with the remaining sauce, for 15–20 minutes, until cooked through and tender. Transfer to a warmed serving dish and serve immediately.

Turkey Salad Pita

serves 1

Small handful of baby leaf spinach, rinsed, patted dry, and shredded

½ red bell pepper, seeded and thinly sliced

½ carrot, peeled and coarsely grated

4 tablespoons hummus

3 ounces sliced, skinless, cooked turkey

½ tablespoon sunflower seeds

1 whole-wheat pita bread

Salt and pepper

Preheat the broiler to high.

Put the spinach leaves, red bell pepper, carrot, and hummus into a large bowl and stir together, so all the salad ingredients are coated with the hummus. Stir in the turkey and sunflower seeds and season with salt and pepper to taste.

Put the pita bread under the broiler for about 1 minute on each side to warm through, but do not brown. Cut it in half to make 2 "pockets" of bread.

Divide the salad among the bread pockets and serve.

Traditional Greek Salad

serves 4

7 ounces Greek feta cheese

½ head iceberg lettuce or 1 head Romaine or escarole, shredded or sliced

4 tomatoes, cut into fourths

½ cucumber, sliced

12 Greek black olives, pitted

2 tablespoons chopped fresh herbs, such as oregano, flat-leaf parsley, mint, or basil

for the dressing

6 tablespoons extra-virgin olive oil

2 tablespoons fresh lemon juice

1 garlic clove, crushed

Pinch of sugar

Salt and pepper

Make the dressing by whisking together the oil, lemon juice, garlic, sugar, salt, and pepper in a small bowl. Set aside.

Cut the feta cheese into cubes about 1-inch square. Put the lettuce, tomatoes, and cucumber in a salad bowl. Scatter over the cheese and toss together.

Just before serving, whisk the dressing, pour over the salad greens, and toss together. Scatter over the olives and chopped herbs and serve.

Smoked Chicken & Cranberry Salad

serves 4

1 smoked chicken, weighing 3 pounds

1 cup dried cranberries

2 tablespoons apple juice or water

7 ounces sugar snap peas

2 ripe avocados

juice of ½ lemon

4 lettuce hearts

1 bunch watercress, trimmed

2 ounces arugula

for the dressing

2 tablespoons olive oil

1 tablespoon walnut oil

2 tablespoons lemon juice

1 tablespoon chopped fresh mixed herbs, such as parsley and lemon thyme

Salt and pepper

Carve the chicken carefully, slicing the white meat. Divide the legs into thighs and drumsticks and trim the wings. Cover with plastic wrap and refrigerate.

Put the cranberries in a bowl. Stir in the apple juice, then cover with plastic wrap and let soak for 30 minutes.

Meanwhile, blanch the sugar snap peas, then refresh under cold running water and drain.

Peel, pit and slice the avocados and toss in the lemon juice to prevent discoloration.

Separate the lettuce hearts and arrange on a large serving platter with the avocados, sugar snap peas, watercress, arugula, and the chicken.

Put all the dressing ingredients, with salt and pepper to taste, in a screw-top jar, then screw on the lid and shake until well blended.

Drain the cranberries and mix them with the dressing, then pour over the salad. Serve immediately.

Barbecued Beef Skewers

serves 4

Olive oil, for brushing
2 red onions
4 scallions
1 pound 9 ounces sirloin steak, cut into cubes

for the barbecue sauce

2 tablespoons butter
2 tablespoons olive oil
1 Bermuda onion, finely chopped
2 garlic cloves, finely chopped
1 celery stalk, finely chopped
1–2 fresh red chiles, seeded and chopped
One 14.5-ounce can chopped tomatoes
2 tablespoons tomato paste
1 teaspoon mustard powder
1 bay leaf
2 tablespoons Worcestershire sauce
3 tablespoons honey
1 tablespoon red-wine vinegar
Salt and pepper

First, make the sauce. Melt the butter with the oil in a pan. Add the onion, garlic, and celery and cook over low heat, stirring occasionally, for 5 minutes, until softened. Add the chiles and cook, stirring occasionally, for an additional 3 minutes. Stir in the tomatoes, tomato paste, mustard powder, bay leaf, Worcestershire sauce, honey, and vinegar and season to taste with salt and pepper. Increase the heat to medium and bring to a boil, then reduce the heat and simmer, stirring occasionally, for 15–20 minutes, until thickened.

Remove the pan from the heat and let cool slightly. Remove and discard the bay leaf, transfer the sauce to a food processor, and process until smooth. Press the sauce through a strainer into a bowl.

Preheat the barbecue or broiler. Brush 4 metal skewers with oil. Cut each red onion into 8 wedges. Trim the scallions and cut in half widthwise. Thread the steak cubes onto the skewers, alternating them with the onion wedges and scallion halves.

Transfer about three-quarters of the barbecue sauce to a sauceboat. Brush half the remainder over the kabobs and cook on the barbecue or under the broiler for 8–10 minutes, turning frequently and brushing with the remaining sauce from the bowl, until the meat is cooked to your liking. Serve immediately with the reserved sauce.

Spare Ribs in Barbecue Sauce

serves 4

2 tablespoons butter
2 tablespoons olive oil
1 onion, finely chopped
2 garlic cloves, finely chopped
1 celery stalk, finely chopped
One 14.5-ounce can chopped tomatoes
2 tablespoons tomato paste
2–3 tablespoons brown sugar
2 tablespoons orange juice
1 tablespoon honey
1 teaspoon whole-grain mustard
2 tablespoons red-wine vinegar
1 tablespoon Worcestershire sauce
3 pound 5 ounces pork spareribs
Salt and pepper
Chopped fresh flat-leaf parsley, to garnish

Preheat the oven to 400°F.

Melt the butter with the oil in a pan. Add the onion, garlic, and celery and cook over low heat, stirring occasionally, for 5 minutes, until softened. Stir in the tomatoes, tomato paste, sugar, orange juice, honey, mustard, vinegar, and Worcestershire sauce and season to taste with salt and pepper. Increase the heat to medium and bring to a boil, then reduce the heat and simmer, stirring occasionally, for 15–20 minutes, until thickened. Remove the pan from the heat.

Spread out the spareribs in a shallow roasting pan and bake in the preheated oven for 25 minutes. Remove from the oven and spoon half the sauce over them. Reduce the oven temperature to 350°F, return the pan to the oven, and cook for an additional 20 minutes.

Remove the pan from the oven and turn the ribs over. Spoon the remaining sauce over them and return the pan to the oven. Cook for an additional 25–30 minutes, until the meat is tender. Garnish with parsley and serve immediately.

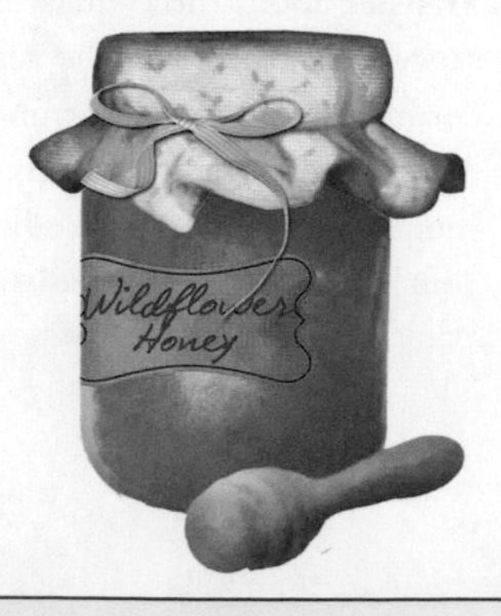

Fresh Tomato Tartlets

serves 6

1 pack (9 ounces) ready-made puff pastry sheets, thawed, if frozen

1 egg, beaten

2 tablespoons pesto

6 plum tomatoes, sliced

Salt and pepper

Fresh thyme leaves, for garnish (optional)

Preheat the oven the 400°F.

Lightly oil a baking sheet.

On a lightly floured surface, roll out the pastry dough to a rectangle measuring 10x12 inches. Cut the rectangle in half, and divide each half into 3 pieces to make 6 even-size rectangles. Chill in the refrigerator for 20 minutes.

Lightly score the edges of the pastry dough rectangles and brush with the beaten egg. Spread the pesto over the rectangles, dividing it equally among them, leaving a 1-inch border around each one.

Arrange the tomato slices along the center of each rectangle on top of the pesto. Season to taste with salt and pepper, and lightly sprinkle with fresh thyme leaves, if using.

Bake the tartlets in the preheated oven for 15–20 minutes, until well risen and golden brown.

Transfer the tartlets to warmed serving plates and serve while they are still piping hot.

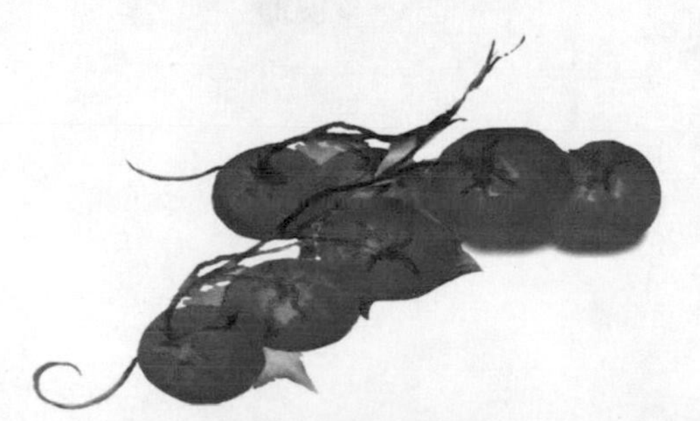

Sicilian-Style Tuna

serves 4

4 tuna steaks, about 5 ounces each

2 fennel bulbs, thickly sliced lengthwise

2 red onions, sliced

2 tablespoons extra-virgin olive oil

Crusty rolls, to serve

for the marinade

½ cup extra-virgin olive oil

4 garlic cloves, finely chopped

4 fresh red chiles, seeded and finely chopped

Juice and finely grated zest of 2 lemons

4 tablespoons finely chopped fresh flat-leaf parsley

Salt and pepper

Whisk all the marinade ingredients together in a small bowl.

Put the tuna steaks in a large, shallow dish and spoon over 4 tablespoons of the marinade, turning until well coated. Cover and let marinate in the refrigerator for 30 minutes. Set aside the remaining marinade.

Heat a stovetop ridged grill pan over high heat. Put the fennel and onions in a separate bowl, add the oil, and toss well to coat. Add to the grill pan and cook for 5 minutes on each side until just beginning to color.

Transfer to 4 warmed serving plates, drizzle with the reserved marinade, and keep warm.

Add the tuna steaks to the grill pan and cook, turning once, for 4–5 minutes until firm to the touch but still moist inside. Transfer the tuna to the serving plates and serve at once with crusty rolls.

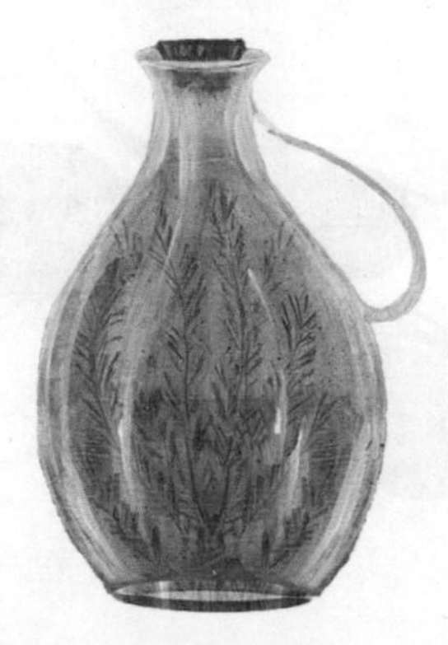

Steak with Tomato and Horseradish Sauce

serves 6

6 sirloin steaks, about 8 ounces each

Olive oil, for brushing

Salt and pepper

for the tomato & horseradish sauce

2 tablespoons butter

2 tablespoons olive oil

1 onion, finely chopped

2 garlic cloves, finely chopped

1 celery stalk, finely chopped

One 14.5-ounce can chopped tomatoes

2 tablespoons tomato paste

2 tablespoons creamed horseradish

2 tablespoons chopped fresh flat-leaf parsley

½ cup water

Salt and pepper

First, make the sauce. Melt the butter with the oil in a pan. Add the onion, garlic, and celery and cook over low heat, stirring occasionally, for 5 minutes, until softened. Stir in the tomatoes, tomato paste, horseradish, parsley, and water and season to taste with salt and pepper. Increase the heat to medium and bring to a boil, then reduce the heat and simmer, stirring occasionally, for 15–20 minutes, until thickened.

Meanwhile, preheat the broiler to high. Brush the steaks with oil and season well with salt and pepper.

Cook the steaks under the preheated broiler for 2–3 minutes on each side for rare or for 3–4 minutes on each side for medium. For well done, cook under the preheated broiler for 3 minutes on each side, then reduce the heat and broil for an additional 5 minutes on each side. Transfer to warmed plates, spoon the sauce over them, and serve immediately.

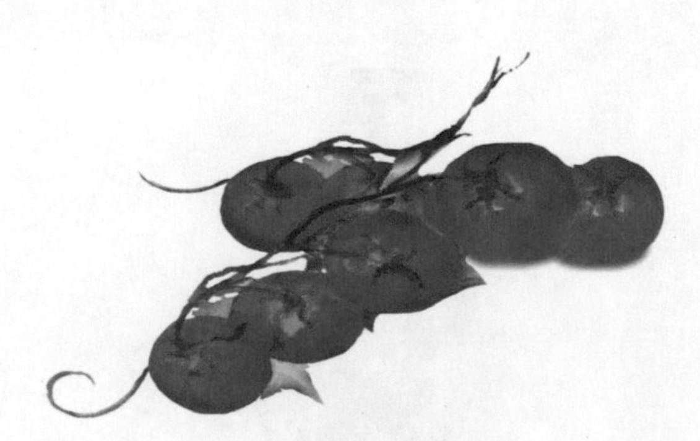

Mussels with White Wine

serves 4

4 ½ pounds mussels
1¼ cups dry white wine
6 shallots, finely chopped
1 tablespoon mixed herbs
1 bay leaf
Freshly ground black pepper, to taste
4 bay leaves, to garnish
Crusty bread, to serve

Mussels should be closed when purchased; if they are open slightly, they should close quickly if tapped with a knife; discard any with broken shells and any that refuse to close. To clean the mussels, scrub and scrape them thoroughly, and gently pull off any beards. Rinse the mussels under cold running water.

Pour the wine into a large, heavy-bottom pan, add the shallots, bay leaf and mixed herbs and season to taste with pepper. Bring to a boil over medium heat. Add the mussels, cover tightly, and cook, shaking the pan occasionally, for 5 minutes. Remove and discard the bay leaf and any mussels that have not opened.

Divide the mussels among four bowls with a slotted spoon. Tilt the casserole to let any sediment settle, then spoon the cooking liquid over the mussels, garnish each bowl with a bay leaf, and serve immediately with crusty bread.

Eggplants Stuffed with Tomatoes & Cheese

serves 4

8 ounces dried penne or other short pasta shape
4 tablespoons olive oil, plus extra for brushing
2 eggplants
1 large onion, chopped
2 garlic cloves, crushed
One 14.5-ounce can chopped tomatoes
2 teaspoons dried oregano
¼ cup mozzarella cheese, thinly sliced
¼ cup freshly grated Parmesan cheese
5 tablespoons dry breadcrumbs
Salt and pepper
Fresh salad greens, for serving

Preheat oven to 400°F. Brush a baking sheet with oil.

Bring a large pan of lightly salted water to a boil. Add the pasta and 1 tablespoon of the olive oil, bring back to a boil, and cook for 8–10 minutes or until the pasta is just tender, but still firm to the bite. Drain, return to the pan, cover, and keep warm.

Cut the eggplants in half lengthwise and score around the inside with a sharp knife, being careful not to pierce the shells. Scoop out the flesh with a spoon. Brush the insides of the shells with olive oil. Chop the flesh and set aside.

Heat the remaining oil in a skillet. Sauté the onion over low heat for 5 minutes, until softened. Add the garlic and fry for 1 minute. Add the chopped eggplant and cook, stirring frequently, for 5 minutes. Add the tomatoes and oregano and season with salt and pepper to taste. Bring to a boil and simmer for 10 minutes until thickened. Remove the skillet from the heat and stir in the pasta.

Arrange the eggplant shells in a single layer on the oiled baking sheet. Divide half of the tomato-and-pasta mixture among them. Sprinkle the slices of mozzarella over, then pile the remaining tomato and pasta mixture on top. Mix the Parmesan cheese and breadcrumbs together and sprinkle over the top, patting it lightly into the mixture.

Bake in the preheated oven for approximately 25 minutes or until the topping is golden brown and bubbly. Serve hot with a selection of mixed fresh salad greens.

Spicy Avocado Dip

serves 4

2 large avocados
Juice of 1–2 limes
2 large garlic cloves, crushed
1 teaspoon mild chili powder
Salt and pepper

Cut the avocados in half. Remove and discard the pits and skin.

Place the avocado flesh in a food processor with the juice of 1 or 2 limes, according to taste.

Add the garlic and chili powder and process until smooth. Transfer to a large serving bowl, season to taste, and serve

Three-Color Salad

serves 4

10 ounces buffalo mozzarella, drained and thinly sliced
8 large tomatoes, sliced
20 fresh basil leaves
½ cup extra-virgin olive oil
Salt and pepper

Arrange the mozzarella and tomato slices on 4 individual serving plates and season to taste with salt. Set aside in a cool place for 30 minutes.

Sprinkle the basil leaves over the salad and drizzle with the olive oil. Season with pepper and serve immediately.

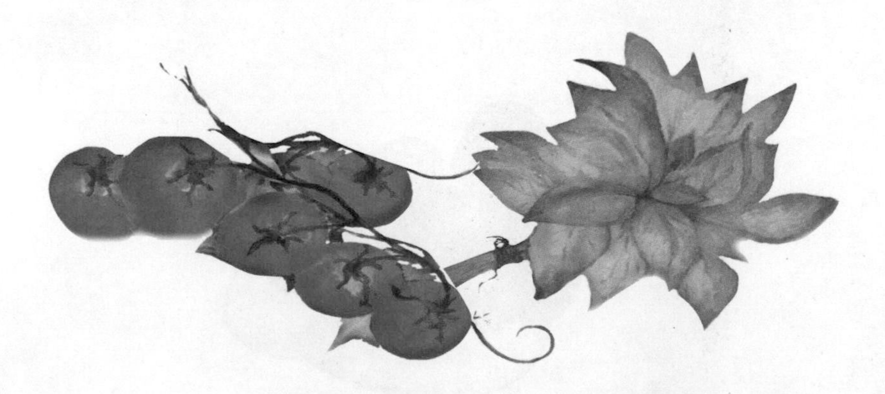

Spaghetti with Tomato and Basil Sauce

serves 4

5 tablespoons extra-virgin olive oil
1 onion, finely chopped
Two 14.5-ounce cans canned chopped tomatoes
4 garlic cloves, cut into quarters
1 pound dried spaghetti
Large handful fresh basil leaves, shredded
Salt and pepper
Freshly grated Parmesan cheese, to serve

Heat the oil in a large pan over medium heat. Add the onion and cook gently for 5 minutes, until soft. Add the tomatoes and garlic. Bring to a boil, then simmer over medium-low heat for 25–30 minutes, or until the oil separates from the tomato. Season to taste with salt and pepper.

Bring a large saucepan of lightly salted water to a boil. Add the pasta, bring back to a boil, and cook for 8–10 minutes, or until tender but still firm to the bite. Drain and transfer to a warmed serving dish.

Pour the sauce over the pasta. Add the basil and toss well to mix. Serve with Parmesan.

Farfalle with Chicken and Broccoli

serves 4

4 tablespoons olive oil
5 tablespoons butter
3 garlic cloves, very finely chopped
1 pound boneless, skinless chicken breasts, diced
¼ teaspoon dried chile flakes
1 pound small broccoli florets
10 ounces dried farfalle (pasta bows)
6 ounces bottled roasted red bell peppers, drained and diced
1 cup chicken stock
Salt and pepper

Bring a large pan of salted water to a boil. Meanwhile, heat the olive oil and butter in a large skillet over medium-low heat. Add the garlic and cook until just beginning to color.

Add the diced chicken, then raise the heat to medium and cook for 4–5 minutes, or until the chicken is no longer pink. Add the chile flakes and season to taste with salt and pepper. Remove from the heat.

Plunge the broccoli into the boiling water and cook for 2 minutes. Remove with a slotted spoon and set aside. Bring the water back to a boil. Add the pasta and cook for 8–10 minutes, or until tender but still firm to the bite. Drain and add to the chicken mixture in the pan. Add the broccoli and roasted bell peppers. Pour in the stock. Simmer briskly over medium-high heat, stirring frequently, until most of the liquid has been absorbed. Transfer to warmed dishes and serve.

Melon and Strawberry Salad

serves 4

½ head iceberg lettuce, shredded
1 small honeydew melon
1 ⅓ cups sliced strawberries
2-inch piece cucumber, thinly sliced
Fresh mint sprigs, for garnishing

for the dressing
¾ cup plain yogurt
2-inch piece cucumber, peeled
A few fresh mint leaves
½ teaspoon finely grated lime or lemon zest
3–4 ice cubes

Arrange the shredded lettuce on 4 serving plates.

Cut the melon lengthwise into quarters. Scoop out the seeds and cut through the flesh down to the skin at 1-inch intervals. Cut the melon close to the skin and detach the flesh.

Place the chunks of melon on the shredded lettuce with the strawberries and cucumber slices.

To make the dressing, put the yogurt, cucumber, mint leaves, lime or lemon zest, and ice cubes into a blender or food processor. Blend together for about 15 seconds, until smooth. Alternatively, chop the cucumber and mint finely, crush the ice cubes, and combine with the other ingredients.

Serve the salad with a little dressing poured over it. Garnish with sprigs of fresh mint.

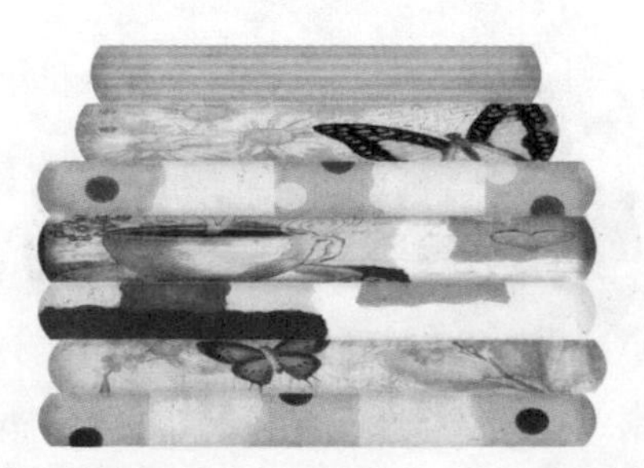

Lemon Pound Cake

serves 8

Butter, for greasing
1¾ cups all-purpose flour
2 teaspoon baking powder
1 cup sugar
4 eggs
⅔ cup sour cream
Zest of 1 large lemon
4 tablespoons lemon juice
⅔ cup sunflower oil

for the syrup
4 tablespoons confectioners' sugar
3 tablespoons lemon juice

Preheat the oven to 350°F.

Lightly grease an 8-inch loose-bottom round cake pan and line the bottom with parchment paper.

Sift the flour and baking powder together into a mixing bowl and stir in the sugar.

In a separate bowl, whisk the eggs, sour cream, lemon zest, lemon juice, and oil together.

Pour the egg mixture into the dry ingredients and mix well until evenly combined.

Pour the mixture into the prepared pan and bake in the preheated oven for 45–60 minutes, or until risen and golden brown.

Meanwhile, to make the syrup, mix the sugar and lemon juice together in a small pan. Stir over low heat until just beginning to bubble and turn syrupy.

As soon as the cake comes out of the oven, prick the surface with a fine skewer, then brush the syrup over the top. Let the cake cool completely in the pan before turning out and serving.

Braised Lettuce & Peas

Serves 4

1 tablespoon butter or olive oil
1 small onion, finely chopped
2 heads of Romaine lettuce
3½ cups small fresh or frozen peas
¾ cup fresh chicken or low-salt vegetable stock
4 tablespoons plain yogurt
Salt and pepper

Melt the butter or heat the oil in a large sauté pan with a lid. Fry the onion gently over medium heat for about 5 minutes, until softened.

Remove any damaged or tough outer leaves from the lettuce and trim the bases. Cut in half lengthwise and arrange, cut-side up, on top of the onions. Scatter the peas around evenly.

Season and pour over the stock. Put the lid on, reduce the heat to very low, and simmer for 10 minutes.

Stir in the yogurt and simmer the vegetables for 1 minute to heat through before serving.

Hawaiian Pizza

Serves 2

2 tablespoons butter
1 tablespoon olive oil, plus extra for brushing and drizzling
1 small onion, finely chopped
½ celery stalk, finely chopped
One 7-ounce can chopped tomatoes
1 tablespoon tomato paste
Brown sugar, to taste
½ teaspoon dried oregano
3 tablespoons water
1 cup diced ham
8 ounces pineapple chunks in juice, drained
½ cup grated Cheddar cheese
Salt and pepper

for the pizza dough

2 cups white bread flour, plus extra for dusting
1 teaspoon salt
½ teaspoon active dry yeast
1 tablespoon olive oil
⅔ cup lukewarm water

To make the pizza dough, sift the flour and salt into a bowl and stir in the yeast. Make a well in the center and pour in the oil and lukewarm water, then mix to a soft dough. Turn out onto a lightly floured surface and knead for 10 minutes, until smooth and elastic.

Shape into a ball, put it into an oiled plastic bag, and let rise in a warm place for about 1 hour, until doubled in volume.

Melt the butter with the oil in a pan. Add the onion and celery and cook over low heat, stirring occasionally, for 5 minutes, until softened. Stir in the tomatoes, tomato paste, sugar to taste, oregano, and water and season to taste with salt and pepper. Increase the heat to medium and bring to a boil, then reduce the heat and simmer, stirring occasionally, for 15–20 minutes, until thickened. Remove from the heat and set aside.

Preheat the oven to 425°F. Brush a baking sheet with oil. Punch down the dough and knead briefly on a lightly floured surface. Roll out into a circle and transfer to the prepared baking sheet. Push up a rim all the way around.

Spread the tomato sauce evenly over the pizza crust. Sprinkle evenly with the ham and pineapple, then top with the cheese. Drizzle with oil and bake in the preheated oven for 15–20 minutes, until crisp and golden. Serve immediately.

Angel Food Cake

serves 10

Sunflower oil, for greasing
8 extra-large egg whites
1 teaspoon cream of tartar
1 teaspoon almond extract
1¼ cups sugar
1 cup all-purpose flour, plus extra for dusting

to serve

2¼ cups berries, such as strawberries and raspberries
1 tablespoon lemon juice
2 tablespoons confectioners' sugar

Preheat the oven to 325°F.

Brush the inside of a 7½-cup angel cake pan with oil and dust lightly with flour.

In a large grease-free bowl, whisk the egg whites until they hold soft peaks. Add the cream of tartar and whisk again until the whites are stiff but not dry.

Whisk in the almond extract, then add the sugar a tablespoon at a time, whisking hard between each addition. Sift in the flour and fold in lightly and evenly using a large metal spoon.

Spoon the batter into the prepared cake pan and tap on the counter to remove any large air bubbles. Bake in the preheated oven for 40–45 minutes, or until golden brown and firm to the touch.

Run the tip of a small knife around the edge of the cake to loosen it from the pan. Let cool in the pan for 10 minutes, then turn out onto a wire rack to finish cooling.

To serve, place the berries, lemon juice, and confectioners' sugar in a saucepan and heat gently until the sugar has dissolved. Serve with the cake.

Steamed Chicken with Chile & Cilantro

serves 4

4 tablespoons butter, softened

1 fresh chile, seeded and chopped

3 tablespoons chopped fresh cilantro

4 skinless, boneless chicken breasts, about 6 ounces each

1¾ cups coconut milk

1½ cups chicken stock

1 cup basmati rice

Salt and pepper

for the pickled vegetables

1 carrot

½ cucumber

3 scallions

2 tablespoons rice vinegar

Mix the butter with the chile and cilantro.

Cut a deep slash into the side of each chicken breast to form a pocket. Spoon quarter of the flavored butter into each pocket and place on a 12-inch square piece of baking parchment.

Season to taste with salt and pepper, then bring together 2 opposite sides of the paper on top, folding over to seal firmly. Twist the ends to seal.

Pour the coconut milk and stock into a large pan with a steamer top. Bring to a boil. Stir in the rice with a pinch of salt.

Put the chicken parcels in the steamer top, cover, and simmer for 15–18 minutes, stirring the rice once, until the rice is tender and the chicken is cooked through.

Meanwhile, peel the carrot, then trim the carrot, cucumber, and scallions and cut into fine sticks. Sprinkle with the vinegar.

Unwrap the chicken, reserving the juices, and cut in half diagonally. Serve the chicken on the rice, with the juices spooned over and pickled vegetables on the side.

Clams in Black-Bean Sauce

2 pounds small clams
1 tablespoon canola oil
1 teaspoon finely chopped fresh ginger
1 teaspoon finely chopped garlic
1 tablespoon black beans, rinsed and coarsely chopped
2 teaspoons Chinese rice wine or dry sherry
1 tablespoon finely chopped scallion
1 teaspoon salt (optional)

Wash the clams thoroughly, let soak in clean water until you are ready to use them.

Heat a wok over high heat for 30 seconds. Add the oil, swirl it around, and heat for 30 seconds. Add the ginger and garlic and stir-fry until fragrant. Add the black beans and cook for 1 minute.

Add the clams and rice wine and stir-fry over high heat for 2 minutes to combine all the ingredients, then cover and cook for 3 minutes. Add the scallion and salt, if using, and serve immediately.

Very Berry Dessert

serves 6-8

One ½-ounce package strawberry-flavored gelatin

¾ cup unsweetened cranberry juice

1 pound raspberries, strawberries, blueberries, and blackberries, plus extra berries for decorating

Make up the gelatin according to the package directions, but use the cranberry juice to replace some of the water.

Place a mixture of berries in the bottom of individual serving glasses or plastic cups and pour over the gelatin. Let chill in the refrigerator for 6 hours until firmly set. Serve decorated with more berries.

To make a striped layer dessert, use 2 contrasting colored gelatins. Place one-quarter of the berries in a bowl and top with half of one gelatin. Chill until just set, then add more berries and half of the contrasting gelatin. Chill as before.

Repeat twice more with the remaining gelatin, alternating the colors. Chill until firmly set.

Fall

Spiced Pumpkin Soup

serves 4

2 tablespoons olive oil

1 onion, chopped

1 garlic clove, chopped

1 tablespoon chopped fresh ginger

1 small red chile, seeded and finely chopped

2 tablespoons chopped fresh cilantro

1 bay leaf

2 pounds pumpkin, peeled, seeded, and diced

2½ cups vegetable stock

Salt and pepper

Light cream, to garnish

Heat the oil in a pan over medium heat. Add the onion and garlic and cook, stirring, for about 4 minutes, until slightly softened. Add the ginger, chile, cilantro, bay leaf, and pumpkin, and cook for another 3 minutes.

Pour in the stock and bring to a boil. Using a slotted spoon, skim any foam from the surface. Reduce the heat and simmer gently, stirring occasionally, for about 25 minutes, or until the pumpkin is tender. Remove from the heat, take out the bay leaf, and let cool a little.

Transfer the soup into a food processor or blender and process until smooth (you may have to do this in batches). Return the mixture to the rinsed-out pan and season to taste with salt and pepper. Reheat gently, stirring. Remove from the heat, pour into warmed soup bowls, garnish each one with a swirl of cream, and serve.

Chicken & Apple Casserole

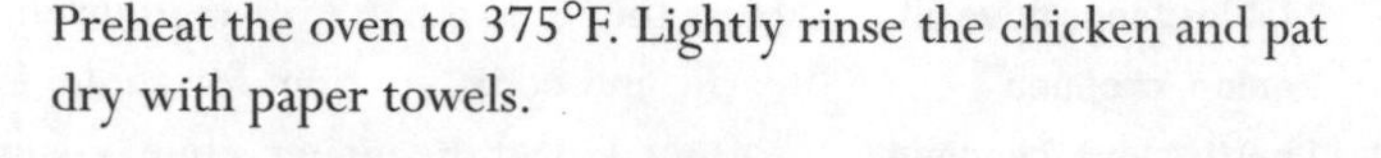

serves 4

4 chicken portions, about 6 ounces each,
1 tablespoon olive oil
1 onion, chopped
2 celery stalks, coarsely chopped
1½ tablespoons all-purpose flour
1¼ cups clear apple juice
⅔ cup chicken stock
1 baking apple, cored and cut into quarters
2 bay leaves
1–2 teaspoons clear honey
1 yellow bell pepper, seeded and cut into chunks
1 tablespoon butter
1 large or 2 medium eating apples, cored and sliced
2 tablespoons brown sugar
Salt and pepper
1 tablespoon chopped fresh mint, to garnish

Preheat the oven to 375°F. Lightly rinse the chicken and pat dry with paper towels.

Heat the oil in a deep skillet and cook the chicken over medium-high heat, turning frequently, for 10 minutes, or until golden all over and sealed. Using a slotted spoon, transfer to an ovenproof casserole.

Add the onion and celery to the skillet and cook over medium heat, stirring frequently, for 5 minutes, or until softened. Sprinkle in the flour and cook, stirring constantly, for 2 minutes, then remove from the heat. Gradually stir in the apple juice and stock, then return to the heat and bring to a boil, stirring. Add the cooking apple, bay leaves, and honey and season to taste.

Pour over the chicken in the casserole dish, then cover and cook in the preheated oven for 25 minutes. Add the bell pepper and cook for an additional 10–15 minutes, or until the chicken is tender and the juices run clear when a skewer is inserted into the thickest part of the meat.

Meanwhile, preheat the broiler to high. Melt the butter in a pan over low heat. Line the broiler pan with kitchen foil. Brush the eating apple slices with half the butter, then sprinkle with a little sugar and cook under the broiler for 2–3 minutes, or until the sugar has caramelized. Turn the slices over. Brush with the remaining butter and sprinkle with the remaining sugar, and cook for an additional 2 minutes. Serve the stew garnished with the apple slices and mint.

Vegetable Lasagna

serves 4

1 eggplant, sliced
3 tablespoons olive oil
2 garlic cloves, crushed
1 red onion, sliced
3 mixed bell peppers, seeded and diced
2 cups sliced mixed mushrooms
2 celery stalks, sliced
1 zucchini, diced
½ teaspoon chili powder
½ teaspoon ground cumin
2 tomatoes, chopped
1¼ cups canned tomatoes
2 tablespoons chopped fresh basil
8 no-precook lasagna sheets
Salt and pepper

for the cheese sauce

2 tablespoons butter or margarine
1 tablespoon all-purpose flour
½ cup vegetable stock
1¼ cups milk
¾ cup grated Cheddar cheese
1 teaspoon Dijon mustard
1 tablespoon chopped fresh basil
1 egg, beaten

Preheat the oven to 350°F.

Place the eggplant slices in a colander, sprinkle with salt, and let stand for 20 minutes. Rinse under cold water, drain, and reserve.

Heat the oil in a saucepan. Add the garlic and onion and sauté for 1–2 minutes. Add the bell peppers, mushrooms, celery, and zucchini and cook, stirring constantly, for 3–4 minutes. Stir in the chili powder and cumin and cook for 1 minute. Mix in the tomatoes, strained canned tomatoes, and basil, and season to taste with salt and pepper.

For the cheese sauce, melt the butter in a saucepan. Stir in the flour and cook for 1 minute. Remove from the heat and gradually stir in the stock and milk. Return to the heat, then add half the cheese and the mustard. Boil, stirring, until thickened. Stir in the basil. Remove from the heat and stir in the egg.

Place half the lasagna sheets in a rectangular, ovenproof dish. Top with half the vegetable mixture and half the eggplant slices. Repeat the layers, then spoon the cheese sauce on top. Sprinkle with the remaining cheese and bake in the preheated oven for 40 minutes, or until golden. Serve immediately.

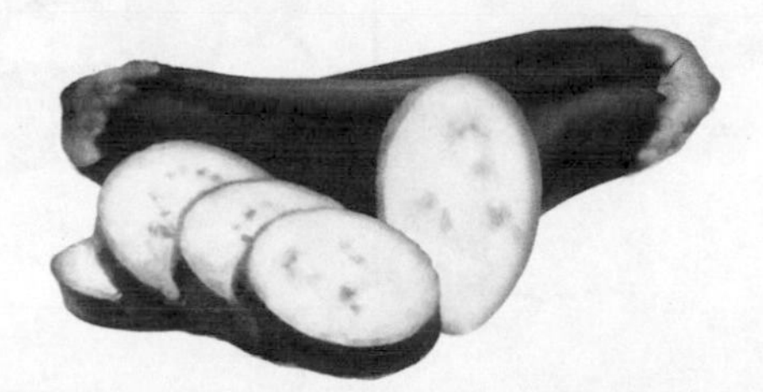

Turkey Steaks

serves 2

2 skinless, boneless turkey steaks
2 slices prosciutto, halved
4 fresh sage leaves
2 tablespoons all-purpose flour
2 tablespoons olive oil
1 tablespoon butter
Salt and pepper
Lemon wedges, to serve

Slice each turkey steak in half horizontally into 2 thinner scallops.

Put each scallop between 2 sheets of plastic wrap and pat out thinly with a rolling pin. Season each scallop with salt and pepper to taste.

Lay a half slice of prosciutto on each scallop, put a sage leaf on top, and secure with a toothpick.

Mix the flour with salt and pepper to taste on a large plate. Dust both sides of each scallop with the seasoned flour.

Heat the oil in a large skillet, add the butter, and heat until foaming. Add the scallops and fry over high heat for 1½ minutes, sage-side down.

Turn the steaks over and fry for an additional 30 seconds, until golden brown and cooked through. Serve immediately with lemon wedges for squeezing over.

Beef and Vegetable Gratin

serves 6

3 tablespoons sunflower oil
2 garlic cloves, finely chopped
2 onions, sliced
2 pounds ground beef
1 pound zucchini, thinly sliced
4–5 carrots, thinly sliced
1 red bell pepper, seeded and thinly sliced
⅓ cup raisins
6 tablespoons butter
¾ cup all-purpose flour
3¾ cups milk
1 cup grated Cheddar cheese
One 12-ounce can corn kernels, drained
One 15-ounce can cannellini beans, drained and rinsed
2 tablespoons chopped fresh parsley
4 egg yolks
Salt and pepper

Preheat the oven to 350°F.

Heat the oil in a large pan. Add the garlic and onions and cook over low heat, stirring occasionally, for 8–10 minutes, until golden brown. Add the ground beef, increase the heat to medium, and cook, stirring frequently and breaking it up with a wooden spoon, for 8–10 minutes, until evenly browned. Stir in the zucchini, carrots, bell pepper, and raisins and season to taste with salt and pepper. Reduce the heat, cover, and simmer for 25 minutes, until the vegetables are tender.

Melt the butter in a separate pan. Add the flour and cook over low heat, stirring constantly, for 2 minutes. Remove the pan from the heat and gradually stir in the milk, a little at a time, until smooth. Return the pan to the heat and bring to a boil, stirring constantly, then cook, stirring, for an additional few minutes, until thickened. Remove the pan from the heat and stir in the cheese until melted.

Stir the corn, beans, and parsley into the ground beef mixture and simmer for an additional 3 minutes, then remove the pan from the heat. Spoon into an ovenproof dish.

Lightly beat the egg yolks in a bowl with a fork, then stir in 4 tablespoons of the cheese sauce. Stir the egg yolk mixture into the cheese sauce and pour it over the ground beef mixture to cover. Bake in the preheated oven for 25–30 minutes, until the topping is golden brown. Serve immediately.

Turkey & Stuffing

serves 8-10

10-pound oven-ready turkey, rinsed and patted dry
2 garlic cloves, sliced
1 orange, sliced
4 tablespoons butter, melted, for brushing
Salt and pepper

for the sausage & fruit stuffing

1 pound spicy Italian bulk sausage
4 tablespoons butter, plus extra for greasing
3 celery stalks, finely chopped
1 onion, finely chopped
6 slices day-old bread, crusts removed and cubed
½ cup turkey stock or vegetable stock, plus extra if needed
1 cup dried fruit, such as currants, raisins, or golden raisins
1¼ cups coarsely chopped fresh cranberries
¼ cup finely chopped fresh parsley
2 teaspoons dried thyme
1 teaspoon dried sage
Finely grated zest and juice of 2 large oranges
Salt and pepper

To make the sausage-and-fruit stuffing, put the sausage into a skillet over medium-high heat and fry, breaking it up with a wooden spoon, until browned. Remove the meat and pour off the fat.

Melt the butter in the skillet. Add the celery and onion, and fry, stirring, for 3–5 minutes, until softened. Add the bread and stir until it starts to brown. Add the contents of the skillet to the sausage. Stir in the stock, dried fruit, cranberries, herbs, and orange zest. Add enough orange juice to make a moist stuffing, and season with salt and pepper to taste. Use immediately or let cool and chill in the refrigerator until required. Bring to room temperature before using.

Preheat the oven to 350°F and grease a baking dish. Fry a little dressing to taste for seasoning and adjust, if necessary. Use to stuff the neck end of the turkey, securing the skin over the opening with wooden toothpicks. Put the garlic and orange slices into the cavity and truss the legs together.

Weigh the stuffed bird and calculate the cooking time at 20 minutes per 1 pound plus 20 minutes. Place the bird, breast side up, on a roasting rack in a roasting pan, smear with butter, and sprinkle with salt and pepper. Cover loosely with foil and roast for the calculated time, or until the juices run clear when you pierce the thighs with a skewer.

Remove the turkey from the oven and let rest, covered, for 30–45 minutes before carving. Meanwhile, cover the dish of dressing with foil and roast in the oven for 20–25 minutes. Carve the turkey and serve, accompanied by the dressing.

Roasted Butternut Squash

serves 4

- 1 butternut squash, about 1 pound
- 1 onion, chopped
- 2–3 garlic cloves, crushed
- 4 small tomatoes, chopped
- 1⅓ cups chopped cremini mushrooms
- 3 ounces canned lima beans, drained, rinsed, and coarsely chopped
- 1 cup grated zucchini
- 1 tablespoon chopped fresh oregano, plus extra to garnish
- 2 tablespoons tomato paste
- 1¼ cups water
- 4 scallions, trimmed and chopped
- 1 tablespoon Worcestershire sauce or hot-pepper sauce
- Pepper

Preheat the oven to 375°F.

Prick the squash all over with a metal skewer, then roast for 40 minutes, or until tender. Remove from the oven and let stand until cool enough to handle.

Cut the squash in half, scoop out and discard the seeds, then scoop out some of the flesh, making hollows in both halves. Chop the scooped-out flesh and put in a bowl. Place the two halves side by side in a large roasting pan.

Add the onion, garlic, tomatoes, and mushrooms to the cooked squash flesh. Add the beans, zucchini, oregano, and pepper to taste and mix well. Spoon the filling into the two halves of the squash, packing down very firmly.

Mix the tomato paste with the water, scallions, and Worcestershire sauce in a small bowl and pour over the squash.

Cover loosely with a large sheet of foil and bake for 30 minutes, or until piping hot. Serve in warmed bowls, garnished with oregano.

Meat Lasagna

serves 6

2 tablespoons olive oil
2 ounces pancetta, chopped
1 onion, chopped
1 garlic clove, finely chopped
1 cup fresh ground beef
2 celery stalks, chopped
2 carrots, chopped
Pinch of sugar
½ teaspoon dried oregano
One 14.5-ounce can chopped tomatoes
8 ounces dried oven-ready lasagna noodles
1 cup freshly grated Parmesan cheese, plus extra for sprinkling

for the cheese sauce

1¼ cups whole milk
1 bay leaf
6 black peppercorns
1 onion slice
2 tablespoons butter
3 tablespoons all-purpose flour
2 teaspoons Dijon mustard
½ cup grated Cheddar cheese
½ cup ricotta cheese

Preheat the oven to 375°F.

Heat the oil in a large, heavy-bottom pan. Add the pancetta and cook over medium heat, stirring occasionally, for 3 minutes, or until the fat starts to run. Add the onion and garlic and cook, stirring occasionally, for 5 minutes, or until softened.

Add the beef and cook, breaking it up with a wooden spoon, until browned all over. Stir in the celery and carrots and cook for 5 minutes. Season with salt and pepper to taste. Add the sugar, oregano, and tomatoes. Bring to a boil, reduce the heat, and let simmer for 30 minutes.

Meanwhile, make the cheese sauce. Pour the milk into a saucepan and add the bay leaf, peppercorns, and onion. Heat gently to just below boiling point, then remove from the heat, cover, and let infuse for 10 minutes.

Strain the milk into a pitcher. Melt the butter in a separate saucepan. Sprinkle in the flour and cook over low heat, stirring continuously, for 1 minute. Remove from the heat and gradually stir in the warm milk. Return to the heat and bring to a boil, stirring. Cook, stirring, until thickened and smooth. Stir in the mustard, Cheddar cheese, and ricotta cheese, then season with salt and pepper to taste.

In a large, rectangular ovenproof dish, make alternate layers of meat sauce, lasagna noodles, and Parmesan cheese. Pour the cheese sauce over the layers, covering them completely, and sprinkle with Parmesan cheese. Bake in the preheated oven for 30 minutes, or until golden brown and bubbling. Serve immediately.

Steak & French Fries

serves 4

4 porterhouse steaks, about 8 ounces each

4 teaspoons Tabasco sauce

Salt and pepper

for the french fries

2 large potatoes, peeled

2 tablespoons Sunflower oil

for the watercress butter

1 bunch watercress

6 tablespoons unsalted butter, softened

To make the french fries, preheat the oven to 400°F.

Cut the potatoes lengthwise into thick, even fries. Rinse them under cold running water and then dry well on a clean dish towel. Place in a bowl, add the oil, and toss together until coated.

Spread the fries on a baking sheet and cook in the preheated oven for 40–45 minutes, turning once, until golden.

To make the watercress butter, finely chop enough watercress to fill ¼ cup. Place the butter in a small bowl and beat in the chopped watercress with a fork until fully incorporated. Cover with plastic wrap and let chill in the refrigerator until required.

Preheat a ridged grill pan to high. Sprinkle each steak with 1 teaspoon of the Tabasco sauce, rubbing it in well. Season with salt and pepper to taste.

Cook the steaks in the preheated pan for 2½ minutes each side for rare, 4 minutes each side for medium, and 6 minutes each side for well done. Transfer to serving plates and serve immediately, topped with the watercress butter and accompanied by the fries.

Pepperoni Pasta

serves 4

3 tablespoons olive oil
1 onion, chopped
1 red bell pepper, seeded and diced
1 orange bell pepper, seeded and diced
Two 14.5-ounce cans chopped tomatoes
1 tablespoon sun-dried tomato paste
1 teaspoon paprika
8 ounces pepperoni sausage, sliced
2 tablespoons chopped fresh flat-leaf parsley, plus extra to garnish
1 pound dried penne
Salt and pepper

Heat 2 tablespoons of the olive oil in a large, heavy-bottom skillet. Add the onion and cook over low heat, stirring occasionally, for 5 minutes, or until softened. Add the red and orange bell peppers, tomatoes and their can juices, sun-dried tomato paste, and paprika and bring to a boil.

Add the pepperoni and parsley and season to taste with salt and pepper. Stir well, bring to a boil, then reduce the heat and simmer for 10–15 minutes.

Meanwhile, bring a large, heavy-bottom pan of lightly salted water to a boil. Add the pasta, return to a boil, and cook for 8–10 minutes, or until tender but still firm to the bite. Drain well and transfer to a warmed serving dish. Add the remaining olive oil and toss. Add the sauce and toss again. Sprinkle with parsley and serve immediately.

Chili Con Carne

serves 6

2 tablespoons corn oil

2 onions, thinly sliced

2 garlic cloves, finely chopped

1 pound 7 ounces ground beef

1 cup canned chopped tomatoes

5 tablespoons tomato paste

1 teaspoon ground cumin

1 teaspoon cayenne pepper

1 tablespoon chili powder

1 teaspoon dried oregano

1 bay leaf

1½ cups beef stock

One15-ounce can red kidney beans, drained and rinsed

Salt

Cooked rice, to serve

Heat the oil in a large pan. Add the onions and garlic and cook over low heat, stirring occasionally, for 5 minutes, until softened. Add the ground beef, increase the heat to medium, and cook, stirring frequently and breaking it up with a wooden spoon, for 8–10 minutes, until evenly browned.

Stir in the tomatoes, tomato paste, cumin, cayenne pepper, chili powder, oregano, bay leaf, and stock. Season to taste with salt. Bring to a boil, then reduce the heat, cover, and simmer, stirring occasionally, for 1 hour.

Add the kidney beans, re-cover the pan, and simmer, stirring occasionally, for an additional 30 minutes. Remove and discard the bay leaf. Serve immediately with rice.

Monkfish, Rosemary and Turkey-Bacon Skewers

makes 12 skewers

9 ounces monkfish fillet
12 fresh rosemary stalks, plus fresh sprigs, to garnish
3 tablespoons Spanish olive oil
Juice of ½ small lemon
1 garlic clove, crushed
6 thick slices turkey bacon
Salt and pepper
Lemon wedges, to serve

for the aïoli

3 egg yolks
4 fresh garlic cloves
Juice of ½ lemon
⅔ cup extra-virgin olive oil
1 level teaspoon mustard powder

Slice the monkfish fillets in half lengthwise, then cut each fillet into 12 bite-size chunks to make a total of 24 pieces. Place the monkfish pieces in a large bowl.

To prepare the rosemary skewers, strip the leaves off the stalks and set them aside, leaving a few leaves at one end. Finely chop the reserved leaves and whisk together in a bowl with the oil, lemon juice, garlic, salt, and pepper. Add the monkfish pieces and toss until coated in the marinade. Cover and let marinate in the refrigerator for 1–2 hours.

Preheat the broiler or barbecue. To make the aïoli, place all the ingredients except the oil in a food processor and process until mixed. With the motor still running, pour the oil through the feed tube until it forms a thick sauce. Transfer to a bowl and set aside.

Cut each turkey-bacon slice in half lengthwise, then in half widthwise, and roll up each piece. Thread 2 pieces of monkfish alternately with 2 bacon rolls onto each rosemary skewer.

Cook under the preheated broiler or over hot coals for 10 minutes, or until cooked, turning occasionally and basting with any remaining marinade. Be careful that the skewers do not burn. Serve with lemon wedges and aïoli.

Crushed Sweet Potatoes

serves 4

1 pound 2 ounces sweet potatoes, peeled and cut into 1-inch cubes

¾ cup low-salt vegetable stock

3 tablespoons cold-pressed extra-virgin olive oil

1 shallot, finely chopped

2 garlic cloves, finely chopped

1 teaspoon dried or 2 teaspoons fresh thyme leaves

1 teaspoon sweet paprika

1 teaspoon crushed coriander seeds

Freshly ground black pepper

Place the sweet potatoes in a saucepan with just enough stock to cover. Bring to a simmer and cook for 7 minutes, or until nearly tender (do not overcook).

Heat 1 tablespoon of the oil in a skillet and stir-fry the shallot over medium heat for 3 minutes to soften. Add the garlic, thyme, paprika, and coriander seeds to the skillet. Stir for 1 minute.

Add the sweet potatoes to the skillet and stir gently for 2–3 minutes, until the potatoes start to break up. Pour over the remaining olive oil, a little salt (only if needed), and plenty of black pepper. Stir for an additional 1 minute and then very lightly crush with a potato masher if necessary to break up the potatoes further. Transfer to a serving dish and serve.

Baked Ham

serves 6

3-pound boneless ham, pre-soaked if, necessary
2 tablespoons Dijon mustard
½ cup firmly packed light brown sugar
½ teaspoon ground cinnamon
½ teaspoon ground ginger
18 whole cloves

Place the ham in a large saucepan, cover with cold water, and slowly bring to a boil over gentle heat. Cover and simmer very gently for 1 hour.

Preheat the oven to 400°F.

Remove the ham from the pan and drain. Remove the rind from the ham and discard. Score the fat into a diamond-shape pattern with a sharp knife.

Spread the mustard over the fat. Mix together the sugar and the spices on a plate and roll the ham in the mixture, pressing down well to coat evenly.

Stud the diamond shapes with cloves and place the ham in a roasting pan. Roast in the preheated oven for 20 minutes, until the glaze has turned a rich golden color.

To serve hot, let stand for 20 minutes before carving. If the ham is to be served cold, it can be cooked a day ahead.

Green Beans with Almonds and Lemon

serves 4

1 pound 2 ounces green beans, trimmed

1 lemon

3 tablespoons olive oil

½ cup slivered almonds

1 teaspoon ground sweet paprika

Salt

Bring a saucepan of lightly salted water to a boil and cook the beans for 3–4 minutes, or until just tender but still with some bite. Refresh under cold running water and then dry thoroughly in paper towels.

Remove 2 teaspoons of the lemon rind with a fine parer, being careful not to remove the pith. Juice the lemon.

Heat a little of the oil in a large skillet and add the slivered almonds. Stir over medium-high heat until they begin to turn golden brown. Immediately take the skillet off the heat, as they will burn quickly once past this stage if left over high heat.

Stir in the beans, the remaining oil, the lemon rind, juice, and sweet paprika, with a pinch of salt, if desired. Return the skillet to a medium heat and stir for 1–2 minutes until the beans are heated through, then serve.

Apple Cake

serves 8

1 pound baking apples
1¼ cups self-rising flour
1 teaspoon ground cinnamon
Pinch of salt
½ cup (1 stick) butter, plus extra for greasing
½ cup sugar
2 eggs
1–2 tablespoons whole milk
Confectioners' sugar, for dusting

for the crumble topping

¾ cup self-rising flour
6 tablespoons butter
½ cup sugar

Preheat the oven to 350°F.

Lightly grease a 9-inch springform cake pan.

To make the crumble topping, sift the flour into a bowl and rub in the butter until the mixture resembles coarse crumbs. Stir in the sugar and set aside.

Peel, core, and thinly slice the apples.

To make the cake, sift the flour into a bowl with the cinnamon and salt. Place the butter and sugar in a separate bowl and beat together until light and fluffy. Gradually beat in the eggs, adding a little of the flour mixture with the last addition of egg. Gently fold in half of the remaining flour mixture, then fold in the rest of the flour until combined.

Spoon the batter into the prepared pan and smooth the top. Cover with the sliced apples and sprinkle the crumble topping evenly over the top.

Bake in the preheated oven for 1 hour, or until browned and firm to the touch. Let cool in the pan before opening the sides. Dust the cake with confectioners' sugar before serving.

Zucchini Fritters

makes 20-30 fritters

¾ cup self-rising flour
2 eggs, beaten
4 tablespoons milk
1 large zucchini
2 tablespoons fresh thyme, plus extra to garnish
1 tablespoon oil
Salt and pepper

Sift the flour into a large bowl and make a well in the center. Add the eggs to the well and, using a wooden spoon, gradually draw in the flour.

Slowly add the milk to the mixture, stirring continuously to form a thick batter.

Grate the zucchini over a few paper towels placed in a bowl to absorb some of the juices.

Add the zucchini, thyme, and salt and pepper to taste to the batter and mix thoroughly, for about a minute.

Heat the oil in a large, heavy-bottom skillet. Taking 1 tablespoon of the batter for a medium fritter or ½ tablespoon of batter for a smaller fritter, spoon the mixture into the hot oil and cook, in batches, for 3–4 minutes on each side.

Remove the fritters with a slotted spoon and drain thoroughly on absorbent paper towels. Keep each batch of fritters warm in the oven while making the rest.

Transfer to serving plates and serve hot, garnished with thyme.

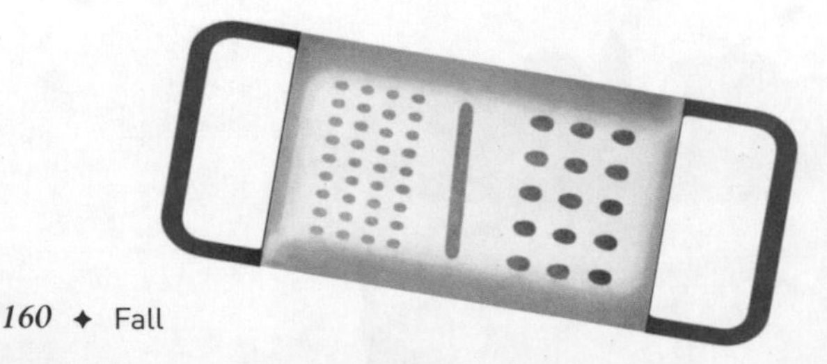

Risotto with Squash and Asparagus

serves 4

7 ounces butternut squash, peeled, seeded, and cut into 4 wedges

1 teaspoon olive oil

⅔ cup finely chopped onion

1 teaspoon crushed garlic

⅓ cup risotto rice

2½ cups low-salt vegetable stock

8 ounces asparagus tips

2 tablespoons finely chopped fresh marjoram, plus extra for garnishing

3 tablespoons Greek-style yogurt

2 tablespoons finely chopped parsley

Freshly ground black pepper

Preheat the oven to 400°F. Spread out the squash wedges on a nonstick baking sheet and roast in the oven for 20 minutes, or until tender and golden brown.

Meanwhile, heat the oil in a medium saucepan over high heat, add the onion and garlic, and cook, stirring, until softened but not colored. Add the risotto, mix, and stir in half the stock has reduced in the pan. Pour in the remaining stock and continue to cook, stirring occasionally, until the grains are tender.

Cut three-quarters of the asparagus into 4-inch lengths and blanch in a saucepan of boiling water for 2 minutes. Drain and keep warm. Cut the remaining asparagus into ¼-inch slices and add to the risotto for the last 3 minutes of the cooking time.

Remove the risotto from the heat and stir in the marjoram, yogurt, and parsley. Season with pepper. Do not reboil.

To serve, spoon the risotto onto warmed serving plates and top with the squash wedges and asparagus. Garnish with marjoram.

Pumpkin Loaf

Serves 6

½ cup (1 stick) butter, softened, plus extra for greasing
1 pound 9 ounces pumpkin flesh
¾ cup firmly packed light brown sugar
2 eggs, lightly beaten
1½ cups all-purpose flour
1½ teaspoons baking powder
½ teaspoon salt
1 teaspoon ground allspice
2 tablespoons pumpkin seeds

Preheat the oven to 400°F.

Grease a 9 x 5 x 3-inch loaf pan.

Pare and skin the pumpkin, then chop the flesh into large pieces and wrap in greased foil. Cook in the oven for 30–40 minutes, until tender. Reduce the oven temperature to 325°F. Let the pumpkin cool completely before mashing well to make a thick paste.

In a bowl, cream the butter and sugar together until light and fluffy. Add the beaten eggs, a little at a time. Stir in the pumpkin paste, then sift in the flour, baking powder, salt, and allspice.

Fold the pumpkin seeds gently through the mixture in a figure-eight movement. Spoon the mixture into the prepared loaf pan. Bake in the oven for about 1¼–1½ hours, or until a skewer inserted into the center of the loaf comes out clean.

Transfer the loaf to a wire rack to cool, then serve, sliced and buttered, if desired.

Chicken and Eggplant Layers

serves 4

4 skinless, boneless chicken breasts, about 6 ounces each
2 eggplants, sliced
4 tablespoons all-purpose flour
1 cup olive oil
1 cup dry breadcrumbs
1 egg
⅔ cup grated Parmesan cheese
Chopped fresh flat-leaf parsley, to garnish

for the tomato sauce

2 tablespoons butter
2 tablespoons olive oil
1 onion, finely chopped
2 garlic cloves, finely chopped
1 celery stalk, finely chopped
One 14.5-ounce can chopped tomatoes
2 tablespoons tomato paste
6 pitted olives, sliced
Brown sugar, to taste
1 teaspoon dried oregano
½ cup water
Salt and pepper

Preheat the oven to 350°F.

Put the chicken between 2 sheets of plastic wrap and beat until thin and even. Cut into 4-inch pieces and set aside.

To make the sauce, melt the butter with the oil in a pan. Add the onion, garlic, and celery and cook over low heat, stirring occasionally, for 5 minutes, until softened. Stir in the tomatoes, tomato paste, olives, sugar to taste, oregano, and water and season to taste with salt and pepper. Increase the heat to medium and bring to a boil, then reduce the heat and simmer, stirring occasionally, for 15–20 minutes, until thickened.

Meanwhile, dip the eggplant slices in the flour to coat. Heat 5 tablespoons of the oil in a large skillet and cook the eggplant slices, in batches, for 3 minutes on each side, until lightly browned, adding more oil as necessary.

Spread out the breadcrumbs in a shallow dish and lightly beat the egg in a separate shallow dish. Dip the chicken first in the egg and then in the breadcrumbs to coat. Heat the remaining oil in the skillet. Add the chicken and cook over medium heat for 2 minutes on each side, until golden.

Layer the chicken and eggplant slices in an ovenproof dish, pour over the sauce, and sprinkle with the Parmesan. Bake in the preheated oven for 20 minutes, until golden. Garnish with parsley and serve immediately.

Apple Pie

serves 6

for the crust

2½ cups all-purpose flour

1 cup (2 sticks) ice cold butter, cut into ½-inch pieces

½ teaspoon salt

7 tablespoons ice water

1 tablespoon cider vinegar

for the filling

6 baking apples, peeled, cored, and thinly sliced

½ lemon, juiced

1 cup sugar

3 tablespoons cornstarch

Pinch nutmeg

½ teaspoon cinnamon

2 tablespoons butter

1 beaten egg to glaze the crust

Preheat oven to 375°F.

Add the flour into the bowl of a food processor, with the regular blade attached. Add the butter and salt. Pulse until the mixture resembles coarse crumbs. Mix the water and vinegar together. Pour half into the processor, and pulse. Add the rest of the mixture, and again pulse until the dough starts to clump together. Do not over-mix. Transfer the dough onto a work surface, and shape the dough into a ball with your hands. Cut in half and shape each half into a disk about 5-inches wide. Wrap in plastic and chill in the refrigerator for 30 minutes.

Toss the apple slices with the lemon juice in a large mixing bowl. Add the rest of the filling ingredients, except the butter, and mix until well combined.

Roll half the dough out on a lightly floured surface to form the bottom crust, for a 9-inch pie with a few inches to spare all around. Place and press into the pan. Pour the apple mixture into the bottom crust. Dot the apples with the butter. Roll out the second half of the dough and cover the mounded apples. Pinch the edges so that both crusts are sealed all the way around the pan. Go around the edge with a fork to make a design, or "crimp" the edge using your fingers. Cut a few slashes in the top crust and brush with the beaten egg. Bake for 1 to 1½ hours, until the crust is nicely browned, and the apples are tender when tested through the slits on the top. If the crust begins to brown too quickly, tent with foil. Let cool before serving.

Orange & Squash Marmalade

makes about 7 cups

7 cups cubed acorn or butternut squash

6 blood oranges, scrubbed

⅔ cup freshly squeezed lemon juice

Small piece fresh ginger, peeled and grated

2 serrano chiles, seeded and finely sliced

5 cups water

6¼ cups sugar

Place the squash in a large pan with a tight-fitting lid. Thinly slice two of the oranges without peeling, reserving the seeds, and add to the pan. Peel the remaining oranges and chop the flesh, then add to the pan together with the lemon juice, ginger, and chiles. Tie up the orange seeds in a piece of cheesecloth and add to the pan with the water.

Bring to a boil. Reduce the heat, then cover and simmer gently for 1 hour, or until the squash and oranges are very soft. Remove the seeds and discard.

Add the sugar and heat gently, stirring, until the sugar has completely dissolved. Bring to a boil and boil rapidly for 15 minutes, or until the setting point is reached.

Skim, if necessary, then let cool for 10 minutes. Put into warmed sterilized jars and cover the tops with wax disks. When completely cold, cover with cellophane or lids, then label and store in a cool place.

Crispy Spinach & Bacon Salad

serves 4

4 tablespoons olive oil
4 strips lean bacon, diced
1 thick slice of white bread, crusts removed, cut into cubes
1 pound fresh spinach, torn or shredded

Heat 2 tablespoons of the olive oil over high heat in a large skillet. Add the diced bacon to the skillet and cook for 3–4 minutes, or until crisp. Remove with a slotted spoon, draining carefully, and set aside.

Toss the cubes of bread in the fat remaining in the skillet over high heat for about 4 minutes, or until crisp and golden. Remove the croutons with a slotted spoon, draining carefully, and set them aside.

Add the remaining oil to the skillet and heat. Toss the spinach in the oil over high heat for about 3 minutes, or until it has just wilted. Turn into a serving bowl and sprinkle with the bacon and croutons. Serve immediately.

Spiced Pumpkin Pie

serves 8

for the pie crust

1 cup all-purpose flour

¼ teaspoon baking powder

Pinch ground cinnamon

Pinch ground nutmeg

Pinch ground cloves

1 teaspoon salt

½ cup sugar

4 tablespoons unsalted butter

1 egg

for the filling

1 can pumpkin puree

1¾ cups condensed milk

2 eggs

1 teaspoon pumpkin pie spice

½ teaspoon vanilla extract

1 tablespoon light brown sugar

for the topping

2 tablespoons all-purpose flour

4 tablespoons light brown sugar

1 teaspoon pumpkin-pie spice

2 tablespoons unsalted butter

⅔ cup chopped pecans

⅔ cup chopped walnuts

Preheat the oven to 425°F. Grease a 9-inch round pie pan.

To make the pie crust, sift the flour and baking powder into a large bowl. Stir in the cinnamon, nutmeg, cloves, and salt, and all the sugar.

Rub in the butter with your fingertips until the mixture resembles fine breadcrumbs, then make a well in the center. Lightly beat one of the eggs and pour it into the well. Mix together with a wooden spoon, then use your hands to shape the dough into a ball.

Place the dough on a lightly floured surface and roll out to a round large enough to line the pie pan. Use it to line the pan, then trim the edges. Cover with plastic wrap and chill in the refrigerator for 30 minutes.

To make the filling, put the pumpkin puree in a large bowl. Stir in the condensed milk and the eggs. Add the pumpkin-pie spice, then stir in the vanilla extract and brown sugar. Pour into the pastry shell and bake in the preheated oven for 15 minutes.

To make the topping, combine the flour, brown sugar, and spice in a bowl. Rub in the butter, then stir in the nuts.

Remove the pie from the oven and reduce the heat to 350°F. Sprinkle the topping over the pie and bake for an additional 35 minutes.

Chocolate Pudding

serves 4-6

½ cup sugar
4 tablespoons unsweetened cocoa
2 tablespoons cornstarch
Pinch salt
1½ cups whole milk
1 large egg, beaten
4 tablespoons butter
½ teaspoon vanilla extract
Heavy cream, to serve

Put the sugar, cocoa, cornstarch and salt in a heatproof bowl, stir and set aside.

Pour the milk into a saucepan and heat over medium heat until just simmering. Do not bring to the boil.

Keeping the pan over a medium heat, spoon a little of the simmering milk into the sugar mixture and blend, then stir this mixture into the milk in the pan. Beat in the egg and half of the butter and reduce the heat to low.

Simmer for 5–8 minutes, stirring frequently, until the mixture thickens. Remove from the heat and add the vanilla extract and the remaining butter, stirring until the butter melts and is absorbed.

The pudding can be served hot or cold, with cream for pouring over.

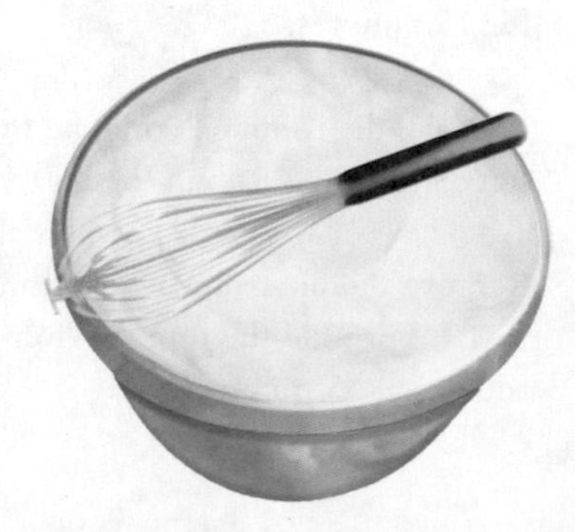

Grilled Steak with Chile Salsa

serves 4

Sunflower oil, for brushing

4 sirloin steaks, about 8 ounces each

Salt and pepper

for the hot chile salsa

4 fresh red habañero chiles

4 fresh green poblano chiles

3 tomatoes, peeled, seeded, and diced

2 tablespoons chopped fresh cilantro

1 tablespoon red-wine vinegar

2 tablespoons olive oil

Salt

Corn salad or arugula, to garnish

For the salsa, preheat the broiler to high. Arrange the chiles on a foil-lined broiler rack and cook under the preheated broiler, turning frequently, until blackened and charred. Let cool. When cool enough to handle, peel off the skins.

Halve and seed the chiles, then finely chop the flesh. Mix together the chiles, tomatoes, and cilantro in a bowl.

Mix together the vinegar and olive oil in a pitcher. Season to taste with salt and pour over the salsa. Toss well, cover, and chill until required.

Heat a ridged grill pan over medium heat and brush lightly with sunflower oil. Season the steaks to taste with salt and pepper, and cook for 2–4 minutes on each side, or until cooked to your liking.

Serve immediately with the salsa, garnished with corn salad or arugula.

Winter

Creamy Carrot & Parsnip Soup

serves 4

4 tablespoons butter
1 large onion, chopped
1 pound carrots, chopped
2 large parsnips, chopped
1 tablespoon grated fresh ginger
1 teaspoon grated orange zest
2½ cups vegetable stock
½ cup light cream
Salt and pepper
Fresh cilantro sprigs, to garnish

Melt the butter in a large pan over low heat. Add the onion and cook, stirring, for 3 minutes, until slightly softened. Add the carrots and parsnips, cover the pan, and cook, stirring occasionally, for about 15 minutes, until the vegetables have softened a little.

Stir in the ginger, orange zest, and stock. Bring to a boil, then reduce the heat, cover the pan, and simmer for 30–35 minutes, until the vegetables are tender. Remove the soup from the heat and let cool for 10 minutes.

Transfer the soup to a food processor or blender and process until smooth. Return the soup to the rinsed-out pan, stir in the cream, and season well with salt and pepper. Warm through gently over low heat.

Remove from the heat and ladle into soup bowls. Garnish each bowl with pepper and a sprig of cilantro and serve.

Parker House Rolls

makes 12 rolls

½ cup milk
4 tablespoons water
5 tablespoons butter, softened, plus extra for brushing
2½ cups white bread flour, plus extra for dusting
2¼ teaspoons active dry yeast
1 tablespoon sugar
½ teaspoon salt
1 extra-large egg, beaten
Sunflower oil, for greasing

Put the milk, water, and 2 tablespoons of the butter into a small saucepan and heat to 110–120°F. Put the flour, yeast, sugar, and salt into a large bowl, stir. Slowly pour in 6 tablespoons of the milk mixture, then add the egg and beat, drawing in the flour from the side. Add the remaining milk, until a soft dough forms.

Grease a bowl and set aside. Turn out the dough onto a lightly floured counter and knead for 8–10 minutes, until smooth and elastic. Shape the dough into a ball, roll it around in the greased bowl, cover with plastic wrap, and set aside for 1 hour, or until doubled in size. Turn out the dough onto a lightly floured counter and punch down. Cover with the upturned bowl and let rest for 10 minutes. Meanwhile, preheat the oven to 400°F and dust a baking sheet with flour. Melt the remaining butter in a small saucepan over medium heat.

Lightly flour a rolling pin and roll out the dough to a thickness of ¼ inch. Using a 3¼-inch round cookie cutter, cut out 12 circles. Brush the middle of a dough circle with butter. Use a floured chopstick or pencil to make an indentation just off center, then fold along that indentation and pinch the edges together to seal. Place on the prepared baking sheet, cover with a dish towel, and let rise while you shape the remaining rolls.

Lightly brush the tops of the rolls with butter and bake in the preheated oven for 12–15 minutes, until the rolls are golden brown and the bottoms sound hollow when tapped. Transfer to a wire rack to cool.

Gingerbread

makes 9 squares

7 tablespoons unsalted butter, plus extra for greasing
¼ cup dark brown sugar
5 tablespoons molasses
1 egg white
1 teaspoon almond extract
1¼ cups all-purpose flour, plus extra for dusting
¼ teaspoon baking soda
¼ teaspoon baking powder
Pinch salt
½ teaspoon allspice
½ teaspoon ground ginger
1 cup finely chopped apple, cooked

Preheat the oven to 350°F.

Grease a 9-inch square, deep cake pan and line it with parchment paper. Put the butter, sugar, molasses, egg white, and almond extract into a food processor and blend until smooth.

In a separate bowl, sift the flour, baking soda, baking powder, salt, allspice, and ginger together. Add to the creamed mixture and beat together thoroughly. Stir in the chopped apples. Pour the mixture into the prepared cake pan.

Transfer to the preheated oven and bake for 10 minutes, or until golden brown. Remove from the oven and cut into 9 pieces. Transfer the squares to a wire rack and let them cool completely before serving.

Johnnycakes

makes 12 cakes

1 cup yellow cornmeal
1 tablespoon salt
1 tablespoon sugar
1 cup boiling water
4 tablespoons reserved bacon drippings or sunflower oil, for frying
Butter and maple syrup or honey, to serve

Preheat the oven to 225°F and line a heatproof plate with paper towels. Put the cornmeal, salt, and sugar into a large bowl and stir. Add ¾ cup of the water and stir to make a thick batter. Gradually stir in enough of the remaining water to make a smooth batter that drops from the spoon. If the batter is too thin, the cakes will fall apart when you turn them over.

Heat a large, heavybottom skillet over high heat until very hot. Melt the drippings in the skillet and swirl around, then pour it into a small heatproof bowl.

Drop 2 tablespoons of the batter into the skillet and flatten each into a 3-inch circle about ¼-inch thick. Add as many more cakes as will fit without overcrowding the skillet. Fry for 1½ minutes, or until golden brown and set underneath. Turn over and continue frying for an additional 1–2 minutes, until golden.

Transfer the cooked cake to the prepared plate and keep warm while frying the remaining batter, adding more bacon drippings to the skillet as required. Serve hot with butter and maple syrup.

Good for You Nutmeg & Cinnamon Muffins

makes 12

Canola oil, for oiling (optional)
5 ounces high-fiber bran cereal
1 cup skim milk
1 cup whole-wheat flour
1 tablespoon baking powder
½ teaspoon freshly grated nutmeg
1 teaspoon ground cinnamon
½ cup firmly packed light brown sugar
⅔ cup raisins
2 eggs
6 tablespoons canola oil

Preheat the oven to 400°F.

Oil a 12-hole muffin pan or line with 12 paper cases. Place the cereal and milk in a bowl and let soak for 5 minutes, or until the cereal has softened.

Meanwhile, sift the flour, baking powder, nutmeg, and cinnamon together into a large bowl. Stir in the sugar and raisins.

Lightly beat the eggs in a large pitcher or bowl, then beat in the oil. Make a well in the center of the dry ingredients and pour in the beaten liquid ingredients and the cereal mixture. Stir gently until just combined; do not overmix.

Spoon the batter into the prepared muffin pan. Bake in the preheated oven for about 20 minutes, until well risen, golden brown, and firm to the touch.

Leave the muffins in the pan for 5 minutes to cool slightly, then serve warm or transfer to a wire rack and let cool.

Pork Chops with Applesauce

serves 4

4 pork rib chops on the bone, each about 1¼ inches thick, at room temperature

1½ tablespoons sunflower oil

Salt and pepper

for the applesauce

4 cups peeled, cored, an diced apples, such as Gala

4 tablespoons superfine sugar, plus extra, if needed

Finely grated zest of ½ lemon

½ tablespoon lemon juice, plus extra, if needed

4 tablespoons water

¼ teaspoon cinnamon

Pat of butter

Preheat the oven to 400°F.

To make the applesauce, put the apples, sugar, lemon zest, lemon juice, and water into a heavy-bottom saucepan over high heat and bring to a boil, stirring to dissolve the sugar. Reduce the heat to low, cover, and simmer for 15–20 minutes, until the apples are tender and fall apart when you mash them against the side of the pan. Stir in the cinnamon and butter and beat the apples until they are as smooth or chunky as you like. Stir in extra sugar or lemon juice, to taste. Remove the pan from the heat, cover, and keep the applesauce warm.

Meanwhile, pat the chops dry and season with salt and pepper to taste. Heat the oil in a large ovenproof skillet over medium–high heat. Add the chops and fry for 3 minutes.

Transfer the skillet to the preheated oven and roast the chops for 7–9 minutes, until cooked through and the juices run clear when you cut them. Remove the skillet from the oven, cover with foil, and let stand for 3 minutes. Gently reheat the applesauce, if necessary.

Transfer the chops to warmed plates and spoon the cooking juices over. Serve immediately, accompanied by the applesauce.

Brussels Sprouts with Chestnuts

serves 4

12 ounces Brussels sprouts, trimmed
2 level tablespoons butter
4 ounces canned whole chestnuts, well drained
Pinch grated nutmeg
Salt and pepper
½ cup slivered almonds, to garnish

Cook the Brussels sprouts in a large saucepan of lightly salted, boiling water for 5 minutes. Drain thoroughly.

Melt the butter in a large saucepan over low heat. Add the Brussels sprouts and stir-fry for 3 minutes, then add the chestnuts and nutmeg.

Season with salt and pepper to taste and stir well. Cook for an additional 2 minutes, then remove from the heat.

Transfer to a warmed dish, scatter over the almonds, and serve.

Pasta and Pork in Cream Sauce

serves 4

1 pound pork tenderloin, thinly sliced
4 tablespoons olive oil
8 ounces white mushrooms, sliced
1 tablespoon lemon juice
Pinch saffron threads
12 ounces dried orecchiette (ear-shaped pasta)
4 tablespoons heavy cream
Salt and pepper

for the red-wine sauce

1 tablespoon olive oil
1 onion, chopped
1 tablespoon tomato paste
¾ cup red wine
1 tablespoon finely chopped fresh oregano

To make the red-wine sauce, heat the oil in a small, heavy-bottom pan, add the onion, and cook until transparent. Stir in the tomato paste, red wine, and oregano. Heat gently to reduce and set aside.

Pound the slices of pork between 2 sheets of plastic wrap until wafer thin, then cut into strips. Heat the oil in a skillet, add the pork, and cook for 5 minutes. Add the mushrooms and cook for an additional 2 minutes. Strain and pour over the red-wine sauce. Reduce the heat and simmer for 20 minutes.

Meanwhile, bring a large, heavy-bottom pan of lightly salted water to a boil. Add the lemon juice, saffron, and pasta, return to a boil, and cook for 8–10 minutes, or until tender but still firm to the bite. Drain the pasta thoroughly, return to the pan, and keep warm.

Stir the cream into the pan with the pork and heat for a few minutes.

Fried Chicken with Tomato and Bacon Sauce

serves 4

2 tablespoons butter

2 tablespoons olive oil

4 skinless, boneless chicken breasts or 8 skinless, boneless chicken thighs

fot the tomato & bacon sauce

2 tablespoons butter

2 tablespoons olive oil

1 large onion, finely chopped

2 garlic cloves, finely chopped

1 celery stalk, finely chopped

4 slices bacon, chopped

One 14.5-ounce can chopped tomatoes

2 tablespoons tomato paste

Brown sugar, to taste

½ cup water

1 tablespoon chopped fresh basil

1 tablespoon chopped fresh parsley, plus extra to garnish

Salt and pepper

First, make the sauce. Melt the butter with the oil in a large pan. Add the onion, garlic, celery, and bacon and cook over low heat, stirring occasionally, for 5 minutes, until softened. Stir in the tomatoes, tomato paste, sugar to taste, and water and season to taste with salt and pepper. Increase the heat to medium and bring to a boil, then reduce the heat and simmer, stirring occasionally, for 15–20 minutes, until thickened.

Meanwhile, melt the butter with the oil in a large skillet. Add the chicken and cook over medium-high heat for 4–5 minutes on each side, until evenly browned.

Stir the basil and parsley into the sauce. Add the chicken and spoon the sauce over it. Cover and simmer for 10–15 minutes, until cooked through and tender. Garnish with parsley and serve immediately.

Ground-Beef Hash

serves 2

3 potatoes, cut into chunks

12 ounces ground beef

1 red bell pepper, seeded and finely chopped

½ teaspoon sweet paprika

1 tablespoon chopped fresh parsley, plus extra to garnish

3 tablespoons sunflower oil

1 onion, finely chopped

2 eggs

Salt and pepper

Cook the potatoes in a pan of salted boiling water for 20–25 minutes, until tender but not falling apart. Drain and let cool.

Meanwhile, combine the ground beef, bell pepper, paprika, and parsley in a bowl and season to taste with salt and pepper. Dice the potatoes and add them to the mixture, stirring gently until thoroughly combined.

Heat the oil in a large skillet. Add the onion and cook over low heat, stirring occasionally, for 5 minutes, until softened.

Add the ground-beef mixture to the skillet and shake the skillet to mix it with the onion, then press down gently with a wooden spoon. Cook over medium heat, without stirring, for 5 minutes, until browned on the underside. Stir well, then cook, without stirring, for 5 minutes. Repeat the stirring and cooking twice more until the mixture is evenly browned.

Reduce the heat to low. Make 2 hollows in the mixture with the back of a spoon. Crack an egg into each hollow, cover, and cook for an additional 5 minutes, until the whites have set. Cut the hash into halves, each with an egg, garnish with parsley, and serve immediately.

Spaghetti & Meatballs in Tomato Sauce

serves 4

2 thick slices bread, crusts removed
3 tablespoons milk
2 pound ground beef
1 garlic clove, finely chopped
½ cup dry breadcrumbs
1 cup grated Parmesan cheese
1 egg, lightly beaten
2 teaspoons grated lemon zest
1 teaspoon dried thyme
2 cups chopped tomatoes
2 tablespoons tomatoe paste
⅔ cup (1 ½ sticks) butter
1 pound 2 ounces dried spaghetti
1 tablespoon mixed herbs
Salt and pepper

Tear the bread into pieces, put it into a large bowl with the milk, and let soak for 5 minutes. Add the ground beef, garlic, breadcrumbs, 5 tablespoons of the Parmesan, the egg, lemon zest, and thyme and season to taste with salt and pepper. Mix well with your hands until thoroughly combined. Shape the mixture into about 30 walnut-size balls and put them on a baking sheet. Chill in the refrigerator for 30 minutes.

Meanwhile, pour the chopped tomatoes into a large saucepan and place over a low heat. Heat gently until warmed through. Add 2 tablespoons tomatoe paste and the mixed herbs.

Melt ½ cup of the butter in a skillet. Add the meatballs, in batches, and cook over medium heat, turning occasionally, for 6–8 minutes, until evenly browned. Using a slotted spoon, transfer the meatballs to the tomato sauce. When they have all been added, cover the pan and simmer for 25–30 minutes, until cooked through.

Meanwhile, bring a large pan of lightly salted water to a boil. Add the spaghetti, bring back to a boil, and cook for 8–10 minutes, until tender but still firm to the bite. Drain, tip into a warmed serving dish, and toss with the remaining butter. Spoon the meatballs on top and pour the sauce over them. Sprinkle with the remaining Parmesan and serve immediately.

Chunky Vegetable Soup

serves 6

2 carrots, sliced
1 onion, diced
1 garlic clove, crushed
12 ounces new potatoes, diced
2 celery stalks, sliced
4 ounces white mushrooms, quartered
One 14.5-ounce can chopped tomatoes
2½ cups vegetable stock
1 bay leaf
1 teaspoon dried mixed herbs or 1 teaspoon chopped fresh mixed herbs
½ cup corn kernels, frozen or canned, drained
2 ounces green cabbage, shredded
Freshly ground black pepper
Sprigs of fresh basil, to garnish (optional)

Put the carrots, onion, garlic, potatoes, celery, mushrooms, tomatoes, and stock into a large pan. Stir in the bay leaf and herbs. Bring to a boil, then reduce the heat, cover, and let simmer for 25 minutes.

Add the corn and cabbage and return to a boil. Reduce the heat, cover, and simmer for 5 minutes, or until the vegetables are tender. Remove and discard the bay leaf. Season to taste with pepper.

Ladle into warmed bowls, garnish with basil, if using, and serve immediately.

Pork with Red Cabbage

serves 4

1 tablespoon corn oil
1 pound 10 ounces boned and rolled pork loin
1 onion, finely chopped
1 pound red cabbage, thick stems removed and leaves shredded
2 large cooking apples, peeled, cored, and sliced
3 cloves
1 teaspoon brown sugar
3 tablespoons lemon juice, and a thinly pared strip of lemon rind
Lemon wedges, to garnish

Preheat the oven to 325°F.

Heat the oil in a flameproof casserole. Add the pork and cook over medium heat, turning frequently, for 5–10 minutes, until browned. Transfer to a plate.

Add the chopped onion to the casserole and cook over low heat, stirring occasionally, for 5 minutes, or until softened. Add the cabbage, in batches, and cook, stirring, for 2 minutes. Transfer each batch (mixed with some onion) into a bowl with a slotted spoon.

Add the apple slices, cloves, and sugar to the bowl and mix well, then place about half the mixture in the bottom of the casserole. Top with the pork, then add the remaining cabbage mixture. Sprinkle in the lemon juice and add the strip of rind. Cover and cook in the preheated oven for 1½ hours.

Transfer the pork to a plate. Transfer the cabbage mixture to the plate with a slotted spoon and keep warm. Bring the cooking juices to a boil over high heat and reduce slightly. Slice the pork and arrange on warmed serving plates, surrounded with the cabbage mixture. Spoon the cooking juices over the meat and serve with wedges of lemon.

Philly Cheesesteak Sandwiches

serves 4

1 French baguette

12 ounces boneless rib-eye steak

3 tablespoons olive oil

1 onion, thinly sliced

1 green bell pepper, cored, seeded, and thinly sliced

½ cup fresh buffalo mozzarella cheese, thinly sliced

Salt and pepper

Hot-pepper sauce, for serving

Cut the baguette into 4 equal lengths, then cut each piece in half horizontally. Thinly slice the steak across its grain.

Heat 2 tablespoons of the oil in a large skillet over medium heat, add the onion and bell pepper, and cook, stirring occasionally, for 10–15 minutes until both vegetables are softened and the onion is golden brown. Push the mixture to one side of the skillet.

Heat the remaining oil in the skillet over medium heat. When hot, add the steak and stir-fry for 4–5 minutes until tender. Stir the onion mixture and steak together and season with salt and pepper.

Preheat the broiler to medium. Divide the steak mixture between the 4 bottom halves of bread and top with the cheese. Place them on a broiler rack and broil for 1–2 minutes until the cheese has melted, then cover with the top halves of bread and press down gently. Serve immediately with hot-pepper sauce.

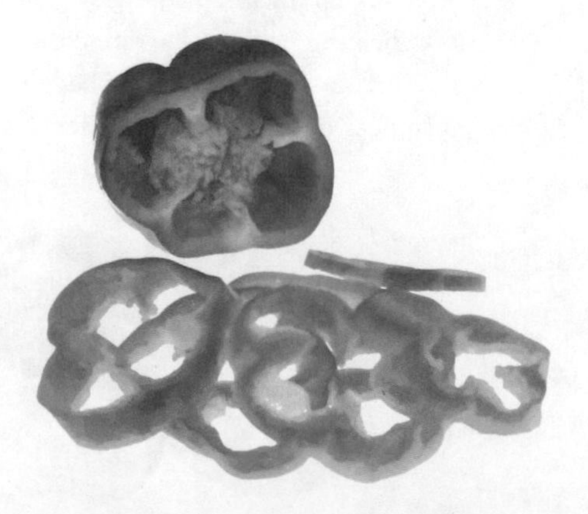

Penne with Creamy Mushrooms

serves 4

4 tablespoons butter

1 tablespoon olive oil

6 shallots, sliced

1 pound cremini mushrooms, sliced

1 teaspoon all-purpose flour

⅔ cup heavy cream

2 tablespoons port

4 ounces sun-dried tomatoes in oil, drained and chopped

Pinch freshly grated nutmeg

12 ounces dried penne

Salt and pepper

2 tablespoons chopped fresh flat-leaf parsley, to garnish

Melt the butter with the olive oil in a large, heavy-bottom skillet. Add the shallots and cook over low heat, stirring occasionally, for 4–5 minutes, or until softened. Add the mushrooms and cook over low heat for an additional 2 minutes. Season to taste with salt and pepper, sprinkle in the flour, and cook, stirring, for 1 minute.

Remove the skillet from the heat and gradually stir in the cream and port. Return to the heat, add the sun-dried tomatoes and grated nutmeg, and cook over low heat, stirring occasionally, for 8 minutes.

Meanwhile, bring a large, heavy-bottom pan of lightly salted water to a boil. Add the pasta, return to a boil, and cook for 8–10 minutes, or until tender but still firm to the bite.

Drain the pasta well and add to the mushroom sauce. Cook for 3 minutes, then transfer to a warmed serving dish. Sprinkle with the chopped parsley and serve immediately.

Pork Chili Soup

serves 4

2 teaspoons olive oil
1 pound 2 ounces fresh lean ground pork
1 onion, finely chopped
1 celery stalk, finely chopped
1 red bell pepper, cored, seeded, and finely chopped
2–3 garlic cloves, finely chopped
3 tablespoons tomato paste
One 14.5-ounce can chopped tomatoes
2 cups chicken or meat stock
Pinch ground coriander
Pinch ground cumin
Pinch dried oregano
1 teaspoon mild chili powder, or to taste
Salt and pepper
Fresh cilantro leaves, to garnish
Sour cream, to serve

Heat the oil in a large saucepan over medium-high heat. Add the pork, season with salt and pepper, and cook until no longer pink, stirring frequently. Reduce the heat to medium and add the onion, celery, red bell pepper, and garlic. Cover and continue cooking for 5 minutes, stirring occasionally, until the onion is softened.

Add the tomato paste, tomatoes, and the stock. Add the coriander, cumin, oregano, and chili powder. Stir the ingredients in to combine well.

Bring just to a boil, reduce the heat to low, cover, and simmer for 30–40 minutes until all the vegetables are very tender. Taste and adjust the seasoning, adding more chili powder if you like it hotter.

Ladle the chili into warmed bowls and sprinkle with cilantro. Top each serving with a spoonful of sour cream and serve.

Roasted Root Vegetables

serves 4-6

3 parsnips, cut into 2-inch chunks
4 baby turnips, quartered
3 carrots, cut into 2-inch chunks
1 pound butternut squash, peeled and cut into 2-inch chunks
1 pound sweet potatoes, peeled and cut into 2-inch chunks
2 garlic cloves, finely chopped
2 tablespoons chopped fresh rosemary
2 tablespoons chopped fresh thyme
2 teaspoons chopped fresh sage
3 tablespoons olive oil
Salt and pepper
2 tablespoons chopped fresh mixed herbs, such as flat-leaf parsley, thyme, and mint, to garnish

Preheat the oven to 425°F.

Arrange all the vegetables in a single layer in a large roasting pan. Sprinkle over the garlic and the herbs. Pour the oil and season well with salt and pepper.

Toss all the ingredients together until they are well mixed and coated with the oil (you can let them marinate at this stage so that the flavors can be absorbed).

Roast the vegetables at the top of the preheated oven for 50–60 minutes, until they are cooked and nicely browned. Turn the vegetables over halfway through the cooking time.

Serve with a good handful of fresh herbs sprinkled on top and a final seasoning of salt and pepper to taste.

Biscuits & Gravy

makes 12

3 cups all-purpose flour, plus extra for dusting
1 tablespoon baking powder
1½ teaspoon sugar
¾ teaspoon salt
½ teaspoon baking soda
¾ cup (1½ sticks) butter, chilled and diced, plus extra to serve
1¼ cups buttermilk, plus extra if needed

for the gravy
1 pound Italian sausage
2 tablespoons beef drippings, pork drippings, lard, or sunflower oil
3 tablespoons all-purpose flour
1½–2 cups whole milk
Cayenne pepper, to taste (optional)
Salt and pepper

Preheat the oven to 425°F and lightly dust a baking sheet with flour.

Put the flour, baking powder, sugar, salt, and baking soda into the bowl of a food processor and blend until blended. Add the butter and lightly blend until the mixture resembles coarse breadcrumbs. Turn out into a large bowl and make a well in the center. Pour 1 cup of the buttermilk into the well and, using a fork, lightly blend until the mixture comes together, adding extra buttermilk, a tablespoon at a time, if necessary.

Turn out the mixture onto a floured counter. Dust a rolling pin with flour and roll out the dough to a thickness of 1 inch. Using a floured 2½-inch round cookie cutter, cut out 12 biscuits. Arrange the biscuits on the cookie sheet, prick the tops, and brush with any remaining buttermilk. Bake in the preheated oven for 15–18 minutes, until well risen and golden brown.

Meanwhile, to make the gravy, put the sausage in a skillet and cook over medium-high heat, breaking up the meat with a wooden spoon, until browned and cooked through. Using a slotted spoon, remove the meat and set aside.

Add the drippings to the skillet and heat. Sprinkle over the flour and stir for 2 minutes. Add the milk, stirring, until the gravy is thick and smooth. Return the meat to the skillet and heat through. Season with salt and pepper to taste, adding cayenne pepper, if using. Split the hot biscuits, then butter them and serve immediately, with the gravy spooned over.

Chicken, Pumpkin & Chorizo Casserole

serves 4

3 tablespoons olive oil

One 5-pound chicken, cut into 8 pieces and dusted with flour

8 ounces fresh chorizo sausages, thickly sliced

3 tablespoons chopped fresh sage

1 onion, chopped

6 garlic cloves, peeled and sliced

2 celery stalks, sliced

1 small sugar pumpkin or butternut squash, peeled and coarsely chopped

1 cup dry sherry

2½ cups chicken broth

One 14.5-ounce can chopped tomatoes

2 bay leaves

Salt and pepper

3-4 tablespoons chopped fresh flat-leaf parsley

Preheat the oven to 350°F.

Heat the oil in a Dutch oven or flameproof casserole and fry the chicken with the chorizo and sage leaves until golden brown. Remove the meat with a slotted spoon and reserve.

Add the onion, garlic, celery, and pumpkin to the casserole, and cook until the vegetables begin to brown slightly. Add the sherry, chicken broth, tomatoes, and bay leaves, and season with salt and pepper to taste.

Return the reserved chicken, chorizo, and sage to the casserole, cover, and cook in the oven for 1 hour. Remove the casserole from the oven, uncover, stir in the chopped parsley and serve.

Baked Beef and Potato Layers

serves 4

¼ cup tomato paste
½ cup water
One 14.5-ounce can chopped tomatoes
1 tablespoon chopped fresh thyme
1 pound potatoes
1 garlic clove, halved
8 ounces ground beef
1 egg, lightly beaten
3 tablespoons butter, plus extra for greasing
2 onions, sliced
1 cup grated Cheddar cheese
Salt and pepper

Preheat the oven to 350°F.

Mix the tomato paste with the water in a bowl, then add to a pan with the tomatoes and thyme. Season to taste with salt and pepper and bring to a boil. Reduce the heat and simmer, stirring occasionally, for 30 minutes, until thickened.

Meanwhile, cook the potatoes in a pan of salted boiling water for 20–25 minutes, until tender but not falling apart. Drain and let cool slightly, then cut into ¼-inch slices.

Rub the cut sides of the garlic all over an ovenproof dish, then grease the dish.

Combine the ground beef and egg in a bowl and season to taste with salt and pepper. Divide the mixture into 6 portions and shape each into a patty about ¼-inch thick. Melt 1 tablespoon of the butter in a skillet. Add the patties and cook over medium heat for 3 minutes on each side, until lightly browned. Remove with a spatula and keep warm. Add the onions to the skillet and cook over low heat, stirring occasionally, for 5 minutes, until softened.

Put half of the potato slices in the bottom of the prepared dish. Cover with the beef patties, then add the onions and sprinkle with half of the cheese. Top with the remaining potato slices and pour over the tomato mixture. Sprinkle with the remaining cheese, dot with the remaining butter, and bake in the preheated oven for 20 minutes. Serve immediately.

Winter Warmer Red-Lentil Soup

serves 6

1 cup dried red lentils
1 red onion, diced
2 large carrots, sliced
1 celery stalk, sliced
1 parsnip, diced
1 garlic clove, crushed
5 cups vegetable stock
2 teaspoons paprika
1 tablespoon snipped fresh chives, to garnish

Put the lentils, onion, carrots, celery, parsnip, garlic, stock, and paprika into a large pan. Bring to a boil and boil rapidly for 10 minutes. Reduce the heat, cover, and simmer for 20 minutes, or until the lentils and vegetables are tender.

Let the soup cool slightly, then purée in small batches in a food processor or blender. Process until the mixture is smooth.

Return the soup to the rinsed-out pan and heat through thoroughly. Season to taste with pepper.

Ladle the soup into warmed bowls, garnish with snipped chives, and serve.

Leg of Lamb Pot Roast

serves 4

3 pounds 8 ounces leg of lamb
3–4 fresh rosemary sprigs, plus extra to garnish
4 ounces lean bacon slices
4 tablespoons olive oil
2–3 garlic cloves, crushed
2 onions, sliced
2 carrots, sliced
2 celery stalks, sliced
1¼ cups dry white wine
1 tablespoon tomato paste
1¼ cups lamb stock or chicken stock
3 tomatoes, peeled, quartered, and seeded
1 tablespoon chopped fresh parsley
1 tablespoon chopped fresh oregano or marjoram
Salt and pepper

Wipe the lamb all over with paper towels, trim off any excess fat, and season with salt and pepper to taste, rubbing in well. Lay the sprigs of rosemary over the lamb, cover evenly with the bacon, and securely tie in place with kitchen string.

Heat the oil in a skillet, add the lamb, and fry over medium heat for 10 minutes, turning several times. Remove from the skillet.

Transfer the oil from the skillet to a large ovenproof casserole, add the garlic and onions, and cook for 3–4 minutes, until the onions are starting to soften. Add the carrots and celery to the skillet and cook for an additional few minutes.

Lay the lamb on top of the vegetables and press down to partly submerge. Pour the wine over the lamb, add the tomato paste, and let simmer for 3–4 minutes. Add the stock, tomatoes, and herbs and season with salt and pepper to taste. Return to a boil for an additional 3–4 minutes.

Lightly cover the casserole and cook in the preheated oven for 2–2½ hours, until very tender.

Remove the lamb from the casserole and, if you like, remove the bacon and herbs together with the string. Keep the lamb warm. Strain the juices, skimming off any excess fat, and serve in a pitcher. The vegetables may be served around the joint or in a warmed dish. Garnish with rosemary sprigs.

Index

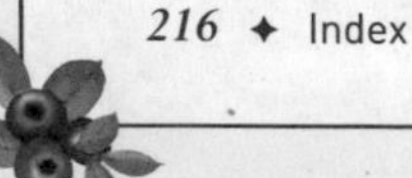